AN UNBROKEN CHAIN

My Journey through the Nazi Holocaust

AN UNBROKEN CHAIN

My Journey through the Nazi Holocaust

by Henry A. Oertelt
with Stephanie Oertelt Samuels

Lerner Publications Company • Minneapolis

"The ultimate measure of people
is not where they stand in the
moments of comfort and convenience,
but where they stand in times
of challenge and controversy."

Dr. Martin Luther King

Lerner Publications Company
A division of Lerner Publishing Group
241 First Avenue North
Minneapolis, MN 55401 U.S.A.

Website address: www.lernerbooks.com

Library of Congress Cataloging-in-Publication Data

Oertelt, Henry A.
An unbroken chain : my journey through the Nazi Holocaust / by Henry A. Oertelt with Stephanie Oertelt Samuels.
p. cm.
ISBN 0-8225-2952-1 (pbk. : alk. paper)
1. Oertelt, Henry A. 2. Jews--Germany—Berlin—Biography. 3. Holocaust, Jewish (1939–1945)—Personal narratives. 4. Berlin (Germany)—Biography. I. Samuels, Stephanie Ortelt. II. Title.
DS135.G5 O376 2000
943.1'55004924'0092--dc21 00-009160

Manufactured in the United States of America
1 2 3 4 5 6 – JR – 05 04 03 02 01 00

Contents

Dedication

The tragic losses of my loved ones and close friends during the Holocaust have always been heavy on my mind. Yet, while writing this book, they all sprang to life before my eyes. It was as though once again, I had been able to spend time with each of them. Although only a few could be mentioned here, there were so many others that were closely intertwined with the numerous events of my life, much too many to write about. These memories will have to remain locked in my heart.

This book is dedicated to all of them.

First of all, to my dear mother, Else, who was murdered at the age of 51 by the Nazis in Auschwitz;

…to my cousin, Stephanie, and to all our other family members, who never returned from the concentration camps;

…to my wife Inge's mother, Erna, who was able to survive the miseries of her incarceration in the camp of Theresienstadt, and had the good fortune to enjoy a good number of years in regained freedom before she passed on;

…to the many members of Inge's and her mother's family, who perished in various concentration camps;

…to the parents of my sister-in-law, Sonja, who, along with many of their close relatives, never returned from the Nazi death camps;

…to the more than two million innocent Jewish children that represent the most painful part of the murdered six million;

…to the countless Jewish families who were murdered, not even having one representative of their families survive the Holocaust at all.

With loving and respectful memory,

Henry A. Oertelt

Acknowledgements

My very special thanks belong to my daughter, Stephanie. Without her encouragement I do not believe I ever would have sat down to write this book. Her help was invaluable not only because of her immediate editing, but also because of her eager assistance in helping me to structure its whole development.

The seed was planted while she was present at one of my lectures as I presented my concept of "The Links that Made Up the Chain of My Survival." She remarked that the audience appeared to be captivated by this idea; a reaction I regularly observe in my deliveries. She, too, found that idea to be a fascinating notion and urged me to put it all down on paper with the intent to write a book, utilizing that image. Her persistence soon convinced me of the importance of recording my past experiences and thus helped me to overcome my fierce reluctance to write.

Inge, my dear wife of over fifty years, was instrumental in saving me a lot of time by patiently applying her secretarial wizardry on the word processor's keyboard. Her opinions and suggestions during that seemingly endless process were very helpful.

Shari, my daughter-in-law, in her quiet, unassuming way, checked everything over again and corrected our oversights. Often she absorbed the material from her point of view, and was able to make some very important suggestions.

After my final manuscript change Corey, my soon to be Ph.D.-granddaughter and computer-maven, loaded everything into her PC only to come up with additional suggestions and corrections. She also supplied me with material providing valuable advice about writing and having books published.

From Portland, Maine, my dear brother, Cantor Kurt Messerschmidt, and his quick-witted wife, Sonja, helped me to clarify some vague points in that often congested traffic of memory lane.

Many thanks to my caring rabbi, Morris J. Allen, of Beth Jacob

Congregation, Mendota Heights, Minnesota, who thought my writings were good enough to allow his personally signed commentary to become part of my book.

Very special appreciation belongs to my good friend, Dr. Stephen Feinstein, director of the Center for Holocaust and Genocide Studies, University of Minnesota, not only for his important suggestions, but also for voicing his confidence in me, even to the point that he contacted publishers on my behalf.

Having had the support and often-voiced enthusiasm of my family was of greatest comfort and encouragement to me. My son, David, and my son-in-law, Eddie, were always helpful and supportive in so many ways.

My grandson Paul, another PC maven, often helped his mom, Stephanie, whenever she got stuck with the intricate demands of her computer.

My other two grandchildren, Sarah and Daniel, always eagerly read every chapter as I produced it, waiting for the next one to be ready.

It's quite clear that I am a very lucky guy and this book is really a product of my wonderful and loving family!

Last and by no means least, I want to thank our good friends of many years, Angie and Gordon Ekdahl, of Alexandria, Minnesota. A good part of this book was created in their comfortable home, by the peaceful beauty of Lake Ida's shores. During the two years of my writing Angie was always interested in the progress I was making, never letting a chance go by without asking when the book would be published.

I am fortunate to be surrounded by so many encouraging friends.

The 18 links described in this book detail the gift of life with which Henry has been blessed.

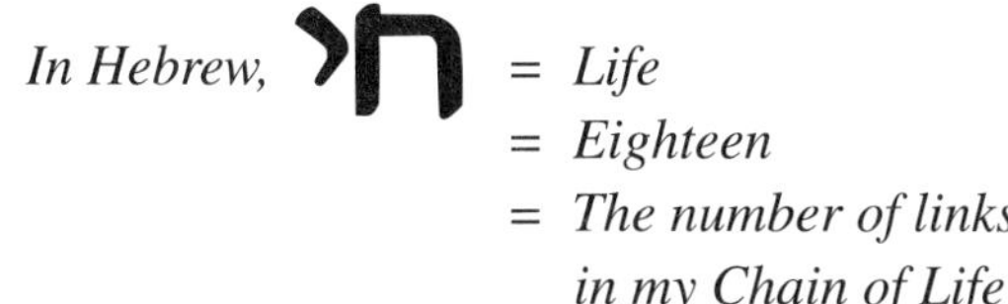

In Hebrew, each letter of the alphabet has a numeric value attached to it. The Hebrew word, Chai (comprised of the two Hebrew letters "chet" and "yud"), equals 18. These letters also spell the Hebrew word for life.

Rabbi Morris J. Allen
Beth Jacob Congregation
Mendota Heights, MN

Prologue

I am a survivor of the Holocaust, one who has been destined to bear witness for its millions of murdered victims. Our numbers are slowly diminishing, but our will to survive and our remaining voices are still powerful. The Nazi system, created to perpetuate inhumanity has tragically silenced so many. Our pointed accusations still ring clear and true and our outcries for justice remain as strong as ever.

There is not a day that goes by in which I am not profoundly aware of the intense effect that being a survivor of the Holocaust has had on my life. It clearly shaped my existence by placing in my way the many horrendous challenges I had to overcome. In my earlier adult years the ordeals of Nazi post-war times and American re-settlement helped to create the colorful panorama of my life. From today's perspective, reflecting back on my 79 years, I am aware that my Holocaust experiences still most significantly influence my perception of who I was then, and who I am now, in a most enriching way. This has provided the groundwork for my life and ultimately for the writing of this book.

I had lived in the USA for at least twenty years before I allowed myself to focus on the details of my experiences during the many years of the Holocaust era. As was the case with most survivors of that dreadful part of history, I had erected a barrier to immediately fend off any approaching thoughts regarding my twelve years of afflicted Nazi persecution. Even so, that blue tattoo on my left forearm (B-11291, 'courtesy' of Auschwitz-Birkenau) was always more than just a subtle reminder. One merely tried to push these images away in order to go on with one's daily life. I never had the desire to discuss the subject with anyone, bluntly discouraging any attempt to be drawn into related conversations.

A very persistent high school teacher and the prodding of the Jewish Community Relations Council (JCRC) caused me reluctantly to abandon my silence. During the ensuing twenty-five years of lecturing and speaking it was often suggested to me that I should write a book about my Nazi-Holocaust experience. I was fully aware that numerous well-written volumes had already been published on this momentous topic, and I originally believed that I had very little to add to the often similar accounts. Yet, throughout the years my audiences have regularly asked the same probing question, "Just how was it possible for you to have endured such horrors?"

So, I would verbally try to describe the many factors that led me through a miraculous maze of circumstances and ultimately allowed me to personally thwart Hitler's evil intent. Not only was I young, physically strong, and often fortunate enough to have been in the right places at the right times, my profession also proved to be of great significance. And there were so many other

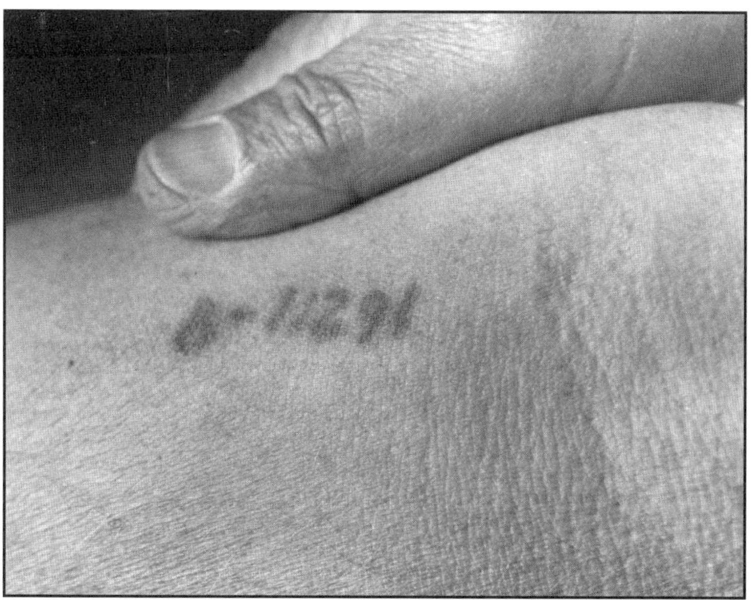

Henry's tattooed prisoner's number — B-11291— on his left forearm

determining factors, each having played a fateful role in my beating the odds in this dangerous game of survival.

A few years ago it occurred to me that it would be interesting to depict the events of my survival in the form of a circular, uninterrupted chain. Each link would represent one episode—or chapter—of my personal experiences in this sequence of my survival. As each incident unfolds it becomes quite clear that if there had been just one weak link in that chain my chances to beat that murderous extermination machine would have been seriously jeopardized.

There were various reasons why I finally decided to undertake this project. Among them was my desire to create an additional personal document that will help to contradict the insane claims of deniers who say that the Holocaust never happened.

For more than twenty-five years I have dedicated my life to lecturing and speaking on this most important subject. As I address my audiences my mission is always clear: to pass on my story so that the world will never forget and will be able to recognize what can happen if hatred and bigotry are allowed to go on unchallenged and unopposed.

It has not been my goal to create another explicit historical account of the Nazi-Holocaust. In general, I have attempted to provide only enough historical background as I find necessary to set the stage for the happenings in my episodes.

I want to point out, that I have no hatred for Germany. That is not to say however, that I ever will be able to forgive the perpetrators, the murderers of the brutal Nazi-regime. I must also say that the greater number of the German Christian population were not too willing to help. Yes, I do understand that this could have meant risking one's life and possibly that of the family. However, it should never be forgotten, that there were a good number of brave non-Jewish people who chose to ignore threats by the Nazis, who saw heart-breaking injustices executed against their Jewish neighbors. In spite of the greatest danger they decided to extend their helping hands.

Among those were my wonderful loyal friends, Richard Föllmer and Fritz Schardin, mentioned in some of the links of my survival. My foreman Kaspar, whose brave actions are also described in another link, certainly should be a highly honored member of this elite group of Christian people. It is established that literally tens of thousands of Jewish lives were saved by such brave and courageous people—not only in Germany.

Not all were able to actually help save Jewish lives. There were those who endangered themselves just as much by trying hard to help make the miserable living conditions for their Jewish neighbors a little more bearable. All these heroic people deserve the ultimate, the greatest and highest honor and respect.

Yet, in the end, there still remains on the sobering bottom line a horrific tally: nearly six million Jews were unable to find a protective harbor for themselves and their children. Totally helpless and abandoned by their neighbors and the world, they were not able to survive the murderous Nazi onslaught.

Introduction

We are a family of Jewish heritage. My only brother, Kurt, and I lived in Berlin with our widowed mother.

Our grandparents died early. The last of them, my grandfather from my mother's side passed away in 1927. I was only six years old. I remember him well. He had a gentle manner that was accompanied by a rich deep voice. His beautiful singing voice was inherited by our mother who passed it on to my brother and me. These strong musical genes are still present in our children and even our grandchildren.

I went to a public school. Three times during the week, after school, I attended a Jewish religious school, which eventually prepared me to become a Bar Mitzvah (full member of the Jewish congregation).

When Hitler came to power on January 30th of 1933, I had just celebrated my twelfth birthday. For years the Jewish population had feared that eventually he would win an election.

From a wide variety of often up to thirty different political parties, Hitler's Nazi organization, under his blustering leadership, had grown from a virtually unrecognized brown-shirted band of thugs into a major political party. Throughout the past fourteen years of relentless hate-provoking tirades he blamed the Jews for everything negative that ever befell Germany. His threats against the Jews were feared but not necessarily taken too seriously. Family members and friends would say things like, "What could he really do to us? This is still a democracy!" My uncle, Adolf, a decorated Jewish soldier from World War I would, along with others, exclaim, "Look, he was just a soldier like we were! We practically fought against the common enemy side by side! He wouldn't and he couldn't do anything to us!" One of the most commonly heard remarks was, "The world would certainly not stand idly by if he did anything drastic!"

One of Hitler's old cronies, the venomous Joseph Goebbels, was soon promoted to the post of "Minister of the (newly created) National Socialist Office of Propaganda." He immediately exercised his new responsibility by escalating the already vicious anti-Jewish propaganda attacks into a much more frenzied and devastating manner than ever before. Possessing a masterful and impressive speaking ability, he warned the German population not to have any contact with these *"Untermenschen,"* or "subhumans," as Jews were now being classified.

In school, in a class of about 30 pupils, our Jewish representation consisted of two, sometimes three students. It soon became obvious that some of our Christian school buddies had become reluctant to talk to us. Many of them had just joined the newly organized "Hitler Youth" movement. There, very quickly and effectively, they were made to understand that it did not behoove a proud member of the "German Master Race" to be associating with a lowly Jew.

It did not take long for the school system to begin applying the newly created anti-Jewish Nazi directives. All Jewish students were dismissed from extra-curricular activities. There were no more field trips, no more visits to museums. I was prohibited from participating in any of the musical programs that I loved and that were so much a part of my life. This was especially sad for me because I came from a family of musicians and was blessed with a decent singing voice. I also was no longer permitted to be a member of the school's soccer team, even though I was one of their best left-defense men.

As part of the newly dictated re-designed curriculum for the classroom it was often necessary for us to read out loud from Hitler's book *Mein Kampf* (*My Struggle*), part of which glorified the supposedly unique and magnificent virtues of the "Aryan Master Race." This part, as well as the other sections that downgraded all other races, and in particular vilified the Jews, did not exactly make me a passionate reader.

All these developments had a quite sobering effect on my enthusiasm for this so-called "institution of learning." I am sure, that these circumstances contributed largely to the reason that I was not particularly wounded when, two years later, I was not allowed to continue my education. I was over 14 years old and did not miss my school very much. Of course, my mother was not exactly thrilled to have a very bored, thumb-twiddling teenager sitting around the house. She was very happy when she found out that the owner of a furniture workshop had consented to accept me for a four-year apprenticeship to train me in the art of designing and building fine furniture.

My brother, older by six years, was still tolerated at the Berlin University. His professors were impressed with his exceptional ability in his multi-language studies. They were influential in retaining him at the university for an extended time, even after all the other Jewish students had been dismissed.

During the following years the dehumanization process against the Jews escalated steadily. The thumbscrews of steadily added constraints were tightened ever so gradually. After every newly announced restriction to our freedom it seemed that things could not get any worse, and that this last one must be the final one of those obscene decrees.

Kristallnacht (Pogrom of November 9th, 1938)

An incident, culminating on November 9, 1938, supplied Hitler with his long sought-after "justification" for striking a devastating blow to the Jewish population.

Herschel Grynspan, a seventeen-year-old student who was temporarily living in Paris, was the son of Polish-born Jewish parents who were residing in Germany. An order by Hitler instigated a forced round-up of people of such background. He had them loaded onto trains in order to "repatriate" them to Poland. The protests of the Polish government were of no consequence.

Herschel's sister, who lived with her parents, informed him that their father had been severely beaten by the Nazis during this ordeal. In his rage Herschel went to the German embassy in Paris where he shot and seriously wounded a high-ranking officer of the embassy, named Vom Rath.

Extra editions of newspapers immediately swamped the streets of Germany. Incriminating headlines reflected Hitler's insanely frenzied accusations that this "dastardly crime was a result of the conspiracy of World Jewry." In his many, increasingly rabid speeches he warned the Jews repeatedly to expect the severest repercussions, should the gravely injured officer succumb to his wounds.

We heard that here and there brown-shirted SA (Nazi storm troops) hoodlums beat up some Jewish people on the streets. It was considered wise to stay at home. The status of Vom Rath's declining condition was repeatedly announced during constantly interrupted radio broadcasts.

We became convinced that Hitler's threats against the Jews were not just idle intimidations, but that something horrible was in store for us if this man should die. But what else could happen to us? Did we not live already under pretty miserable conditions? In the face of such fear it seemed understandable that some Jews actually prayed for this Nazi's survival.

Late in the day of November 9th, over somber Wagnerian background music, the radio announced Vom Rath's death. Once again, excessively large newspaper headlines shouted, "EXTRA! EXTRA!" bombarding the readers with dramatically printed anti-Jewish accusations, flooding the streets of Germany and the recently annexed Austria.

Around midnight my mother proceeded to prepare our apartment for bedtime. She began to draw the curtains but suddenly beckoned my brother and me to take a look through the window.

"Just look at that red sky! There must be a fire nearby," she uttered with a hint of amazement in her voice. We waited to hear sirens of fire engines, but there were none. When all remained quiet we said "good night" and went to bed. Wondering why the sky was so red, we fell asleep.

The next morning I bicycled as usual to my workplace, my furniture workshop. Suddenly I could ride no further and had to climb off my bike! I was forced to pick it up and carry it with its crossbar on my shoulder. I carefully wove my way through the shards of shattered glass that were strewn everywhere. The few Jewish-owned stores in the neighborhood had been ransacked and demolished. Parts of their now damaged merchandise mingled here and there with the splintered fragments of their once shiny display shelves. My eyes surveyed the destruction with disbelief. I tried, without much success, to avoid crunching on the broken glass.

A few blocks away the inside of my family's synagogue had been completely demolished. All the holy items had been trampled on and torn into pieces. All windows, some of them made of beautiful stained glass, had been smashed. There was nothing but glass wherever I stepped. Later on, I learned that the building itself had been spared from being burned because some private, non-Jewish-owned apartment houses were too dangerously close to its structure.

We discovered that late during that night the brown-shirted SA-troops and their black-uniformed SS (originally Hitler's personal guard) buddies had systematically created a night of unparalleled destruction against Jews and their properties.

The long established system of registration of every person living in the jurisdiction of the particular police precinct played easily into the hands of the Nazis. These records contained all the details—race, religion, profession, as well as birth dates. It was therefore not too difficult for them to prepare a list of 30,000 Jewish men. By dawn, Nazis had rounded up and transported these men to concentration camps.

Across all of Germany and annexed Austria, almost all synagogues and Jewish community centers were either destroyed by

Bildarchive Preussischer Kulturbesity, Berlin

Two views of one of the famous synagogues in Berlin, the *Fasanenstrasse*, before (left) and after (right) the destruction of "Kristallnacht."

A close-up of "Kristallnacht" destruction showing Torah scrolls wrenched from their covers, torn and abused.

It seems rather ironic that one of the few lesser-damaged items in the "Kristallnacht" inferno was a Jewish stone carrying the inscription, "Thou shalt love thy neighbor as thyself." (Fasanenstrasse Synagogue)

fire or severely damaged and vandalized.

During that night thirty-six Jews were killed and many more were injured. Hundreds of Jewish-owned shops, department stores and businesses were demolished and ransacked. It was all too well prepared. One of the reasons that these properties were so easily identified was that about two years before, the Jewish proprietors were ordered to exhibit their names, in big white letters on their entrances or the display windows.

The terrifying happenings of this ghoulish night, the *Kristallnacht,* are considered to be the prelude to the Holocaust. The SS began picking up Jewish families from their homes and were sending them to one of the numerous concentration camps that had sprung up like mushrooms all over Germany since the beginning of Hitler's rule.

Some newspaper reporters of the international press wrote about the horrifying occurrences that took place during that night throughout Germany and Austria. But as Hitler had experienced in previous incidents, no world government lodged any serious condemnation strong enough to cause him concern.

He had tested and challenged the world many times. There was not too much of a reaction from other countries when Hitler, against the Peace Treaty of Versailles, reopened all the factories that produced warplanes, war ships, tanks and other heavy war equipment in 1933. The outside world showed little reaction when Hitler, on March 7, 1936, marched into the 100 kilometer demilitarized Rheinland-Zone, which also represented a breach of a part of the same treaty. On March 13, 1938, Hitler annexed Austria to Germany. On September 29th of the same year he claimed and snatched the Sudetenland, a section of Czechoslovakia, all with the official sanction of Britain and France!

Only ten months had gone by since the nightmares of *Kristallnacht* with its massive destruction of Jewish life, freedom and property. On September 1, 1939, the risk did not seem too excessive to Hitler when he gave the marching orders for his troops to violate the

Polish borders, thus signaling the beginning of World War II.

Slave Labor

Within a month or two of Hitler's attack on Poland nearly every man, unless he was Jewish, had been inducted into the *Wehrmacht* (military forces). Jewish men immediately received the military classification of *untauglich für Militärdienst* (unfit for military service).

There was now a serious shortage in the supply of all kinds of laborers. To help alleviate the problem, every Jewish man or woman, currently employed or not, was ordered to report at once to one of the specified employment offices from where they were assigned to one of a variety of work places. Exceptions were made for a few Jewish doctors and dentists, but they were allowed to treat Jewish patients only.

Jewish lawyers were no longer permitted to practice their profession.Therefore, they were among the men who were usually assigned to work at road and railroad construction sites. Jewish women were ordered to labor in factories that produced ammunition or other military components or to sew and repair military uniforms.

All these jobs were performed under severe forced labor conditions. Jewish workers were not given the choice of accepting or rejecting the assigned job. In most cases the groups of these Jewish laborers worked separately from other work crews. Their wages were only one half of what conventional work forces were receiving. Employers were not able to enjoy the difference for their own benefit. In order to show their appreciation for having received a crew of workers, albeit a group of Jews, the withheld money had to be turned over to the Nazi coffers.

At that time I had just finished my apprenticeship in designing and building fine furniture. I had been looking forward to pursuing my profession when I received orders to report to the Berlin Unemployment Office for Jews. It was located in Neukölln, a part

Bildarchive Preussischer Kulturbesity, Berlin

Henry frequented this Jewish-owned pastry cafe, Cafe Dobrin, shown here after it was destroyed on "Kristallnacht." It became Henry's favorite hangout because it was forbidden for Jews to be at any other public places. The Jewish owner, Isidor Dobrin, served "Ersatz-Kaffee" or flavored charged water. The picture shows the broken windows in front of the pulled-down shades. Above the entrance (middle of picture) the name of the owner is clearly visible. Its display was mandatory for Jewish proprietors only. Even the size, type of lettering and color (white) were directed by the Nazis.

of Berlin quite a few miles away from where I lived. After hours and hours of waiting I was assigned to work for a road construction company along with a large group of other Jewish men.

Not to be allowed to practice my profession anymore was a great disappointment to me. However, the physical aspect of this rugged construction work did not bother me. I was young, not yet nineteen years old. My apprenticeship had included a lot of hard, physical activity. Often I had to pile stacks of lumber and frequently was required to carry, load, and unload heavy furniture. But I would have much rather made use of what I had learned.

Also, I just could not help but feel sorry for some of the older men who were pulled out of their offices or business facilities. They were not used to this kind of hard physical labor and often appeared to be very uncoordinated. Under the ration-card system typical work clothing was not available for Jews. It certainly was a quite unusual, almost comical, sight to find people on construction sites often wearing conservatively styled business-type suits. This, of course, only enhanced the purposely-created ridiculous image in the eyes of the passersby.

We were equipped with a pick-ax that needed to be slammed into the hardened ground with all of one's strength in order to break loose big chunks of earth. Our only other piece of equipment was a shovel. A strong push of the foot forced it into the ground. Now piled high with dirt, a forceful swing was required to throw the shovel's load onto a wagon or lorry placed a few feet away from us. The mostly crude, barrel-chested foremen, many of whom sported an alcohol-reddened proboscis, often yelled and screamed when someone was not able to fill the shovel to their satisfaction.

My Christian friend, Fritz, knew about the treatment I was exposed to under these rough working conditions. He told me that he would try to arrange for me to work for his road construction company, which would put me under his immediate supervision. In spite of my warning that he could get into trouble if he did this he went to the authorities to get permission to transfer me to his work site. Not only did they refuse his request, but he also had to submit to a severe lecture about why it was important to stay away from Jews.

Over the following two-and-a-half years I was transferred from one work site to another whenever a job was finished. This necessitated occasionally changing employers.

After a day of hard labor I still was able to return to my family's flat in our big apartment building. Yet, the living conditions for the Jewish population had become increasingly difficult. The systematic process of denying us all privileges of citizenship had begun to rear its ugly head already the very moment Hitler came to power in January of 1933. Gradually, within a few years, the many restrictions applied to Jews had taken on shocking dimensions.

We were sure that the supposedly civilized world would not allow this to go on much longer. We waited for a miracle to happen. But Hitler had tested the world so many times. There was no need for him to change his policies.

When the Allies finally decided to oppose the Nazis militarily, we became convinced that the Nazi-forces would be defeated very quickly and we would be free again. Little did we know that we would have to wait during a long and increasingly miserable time.

The Yellow Star

On September 15, 1941, it was decreed that all Jews had to wear a yellow star, made from fine cloth, on their outer garments for easy visual identification. Its size was about four inches from the top point to the bottom point. The vivid bright yellow background color made it noticeable even from far away. In strange looking, fat black Hebraicized hieroglyphics the word *Jude* (Jew) was brandished across the middle of the star.

The instructions for applying the cloth star warned that it was to be tightly sewn on with close, small stitches. Sometimes it happened that 'offenders' had been spotted with one corner of their star coming loose or with a few missed stitches. Such a 'violation' served as a perfect excuse for a person to be dragged to Gestapo (Secret State Police) headquarters from which the only way out led directly to a concentration camp.

The same type of star was also made from a thin cellophane-like material. Its shiny back, when made wet, turned it into sticky glue, and thus was stuck onto the entrance door of every Jewish home. This action not only accentuated the vulnerability of that home, it also made it much easier for the SS when they were hunting for Jews to be picked up.

The infamous yellow star

Until this point I had occasionally dared to sneak into places that were prohibited for Jews to enter. I refused to be burdened by the choking restrictions declared by the Nazi authorities. An occasional forbidden visit to a restaurant, movie theater or a sports event in a different neighborhood from where I lived not only was a welcome and needed form of entertainment, but created also a feeling of resistance in me.

My mother was always trying to discourage such adventures. Her objections became more frantic after she found out about an incident where a Jewish person was recognized by someone, taken in by the Gestapo and never heard from again. She was relieved to notice that since the required wearing of the star I had stopped my dangerous activities.

But after about a week or two I started again to feel unjustly fenced in. I felt this stupid star made me a marked person, and robbed me of my freedom to move about unnoticed. I started to rebel. If only there was a way to have a star that could be easily removed and replaced without cumbersome stitching, I reasoned, I might be able to resume my 'illegal' activities.

So, I went to work and cut the exact form of a star from an opened and flattened tin can. I spread some glue on one side of this metal star and carefully pressed one of the yellow cloth stars onto it. On the back of the tin star I soldered a long, thin pin that would allow me to leave the premises, sporting that star, looking like any other good law-abiding Jew. When I was far away and felt safe enough, I could easily remove it with just a flip of my hand, only to reverse this action on my way home.

I was fully aware of how dangerous it would be for me to be caught with this device. I was young and was sure that I would be alert and careful enough to avoid any such potentially disastrous encounter. The only thing that I regret deeply is that my adventuresome activity caused great fear and worrisome pain for my mother every time I left the house.

Accelerated Dehumanization

Ever since the beginning of the war in 1939 the distribution of food was restricted through the use of ration cards. In order to receive such a card it was necessary to present our folded ID document. For the purpose of quick pre-identification, and unlike the non-Jewish population, ours brandished a big, black 'J' (for "Jew") right on the front of it. As it was unfolded, another image of a big 'J' appeared. To ensure with yet even more absolute certainty that the ID holder was identified as a Jewish person, the by now mandatory middle-name *Israel* for men, and *Sara* for women, was displayed, inserted between the first and the last name. Because people with anti-Semitic tendencies had been using these names toward Jews only with derogatory meaning, the

Henry (right) and friend in Berlin during the War — without star, with the bicycle that was his means of transportation.

ridiculing effect of 'officializing' its use was fully intended. No non-Jewish person was given these names during those times.

Not only did our food allowance consist of only fifty percent of what the non-Jewish population received, but our ration cards also displayed a large "J" stamped right in the middle of it. This way, the merchant would be warned not to hand out any of the occasionally declared additional food items for which Jews were not eligible. Many Christian-owned stores and businesses kept any potential Jewish customers from entering their premises by displaying signs at the entrances or windows with the warning *Juden unerwünscht* (Jews unwanted).

In March of 1933, within two months of the start of his regime, Hitler opened his first concentration camp at Dachau, near Munich. From then on additional camps opened their gates in various areas of Germany. It had become known that people who opposed

Hitler's regime, sometimes with just a critical remark, were sent to these places. Only the slightest offense, even such as jaywalking, was often reason enough for a Jewish person to be taken to Gestapo headquarters. As always, the usual route from there led to one of the many concentration camps. Soon everyone was aware that the ears of the Gestapo seemed to be everywhere. I remember people in Berlin stopping themselves in mid-sentence saying, "I better not say anymore or I'll also wind up in Sachsenhausen (a concentration camp near Berlin)."

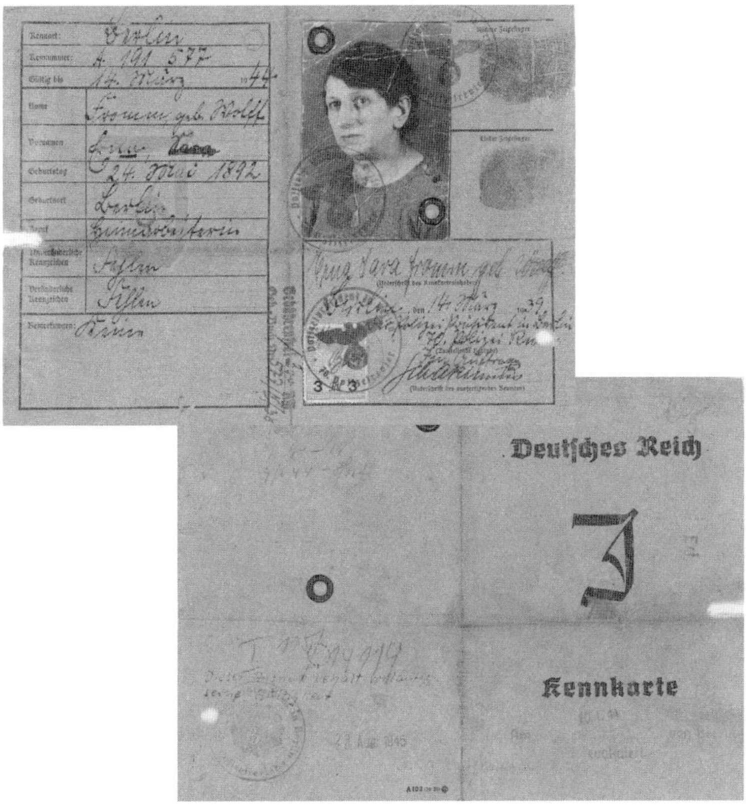

German passport of Henry's mother-in-law, Erna Fromm. The Nazis demanded every Jewish woman be photographed showing her left ear and bearing the middle name, Sara. Jewish men had to use the middle name, Israel.

The number of these camps had significantly increased since the Nazis' invasion of Poland and other European countries. Most of the concentration camps created on the sites of occupied Eastern Europe became known by their odious distinction as "extermination camps."

For Jews it was not only forbidden to frequent any of the restaurants or movie theaters, concert halls and sports arenas, but even parks and beaches were soon declared "off limits" for us. Eventually, Jews were ordered to give up their radios and record players along with any records they possessed. Under cover of midnight, in order to minimize the chance of being detected by some ill-meaning Nazi neighbors of ours, occasionally my wonderful friend Richard would sneak into our apartment building.

It was very dangerous for him because Hitler had warned that anybody caught in the act of associating with Jews would be prosecuted and charged with treason. In spite of his awareness of the extremely menacing situation he would arrive at our door with a bag of food items under one arm and a record player under the other. (The smallest record player at that time was an awkward, manually operated box, about 20x12x8 inches.) This by no means inconspicuous contraption also contained two or three of the thick '78' records that were then in style. The question that comes to mind is why a Christian person would place himself in such peril?

The answer is that Richard realized that we were deprived of two of the most important ingredients of life, the two that he himself cherished most. These consisted of having enough to eat, and the enjoyment of good music.

As we seated ourselves around the dining room table with the record player placed in the center of it, he would turn the crank to wind it up, after which he placed one of the records on the turntable. It could have been dangerous for us if our forbidden 'concert' were overheard by any of our Nazi neighbors. We therefore lowered the sound level as much as possible. For added safety we put a blanket in tent-like fashion over our heads as we sat around the table.

Listening to some beautiful recordings of our favorite operas or classical concert performances was by now a rare treat for us. In spite of the fact that Richard certainly was familiar with the music and could listen to it openly anytime, even with full strength sound and beauty, he would join us with his head also right under the blanket.

Resistance

The question of why the Jewish people did not fight back has always been raised. Well, they did! There were many Jews who were active as partisan fighters. A good number of others participated in underground activities. Among them was one of my best friends and his wife, Heinz and Marianne Joachim. As members of what became known as the *Gruppe Baum* (Group Baum—Baum being the name of the leader) they were seized by the Gestapo and were executed in the infamous prison of Plötzensee in Berlin. Both their pictures and a moving last letter to her husband, written from her prison cell are published in a book, entitled *Jugend im Berliner Widerstand* (Youth in the Berlin Resistance). It was printed in 1978 in what was then the country of the DDR *(Deutsche Democratische Republik,* East Germany). It is interesting to note that there is no mention of the fact that this group of underground-resistance fighters consisted almost exclusively of Jews.

A number of uprisings took place in several ghettoes and concentration camps. The most celebrated of them was the uprising in the Warsaw ghetto on April 19, 1943. It lasted for 28 days. Jews conducted all of these, mostly without any military training. Other smaller uprisings took place in several other camps, among them the dramatic breakout from Sobibor on October 14, 1943. Even the camps of Treblinka, Maidanek and Auschwitz reported incidents of altercations against the Nazi oppressors. Of course, there was never the illusion among these desperate rioters that they

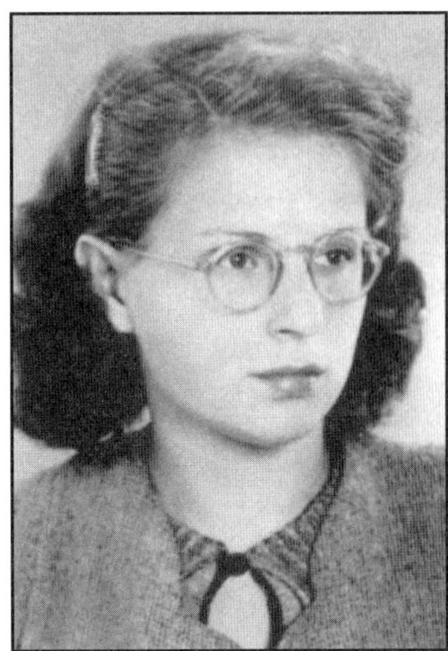

Henry's closest friend, Heinz Joachim and his wife, Marianne, Jewish members of the Berlin underground until their capture and execution by the Gestapo

could be victorious over the well-tuned Nazi military forces. The only hope these brave fighters had was that the outside world would come to support them by at least supplying them with some of the weaponry that they so desperately needed. They soon learned that this hope was merely a pipe dream.

It has been established that another recognized form of opposition was "passive resistance." Every survivor falls into this category, representing merely the fact that he/she was able to overcome the formidable odds against them, in spite of the evil plans and intentions of their tyrants.

It is in this spirit that my book is written.

The Spirit of Survival

Most of us survivors can identify strongly with the links in each of our own individual chains, created as our individual situations evolved. We all had many fortunate breaks that helped us not only to endure, but also to triumph over the countless life-threatening adversities.

Yet, there were about six million Jews who perished in concentration camps and ghettoes. Each one of them had also tried desperately to cope in their own way with their situations. Sadly, it became clear that at least one of their links was not strong enough to withstand the sheer inhuman strain placed upon it.

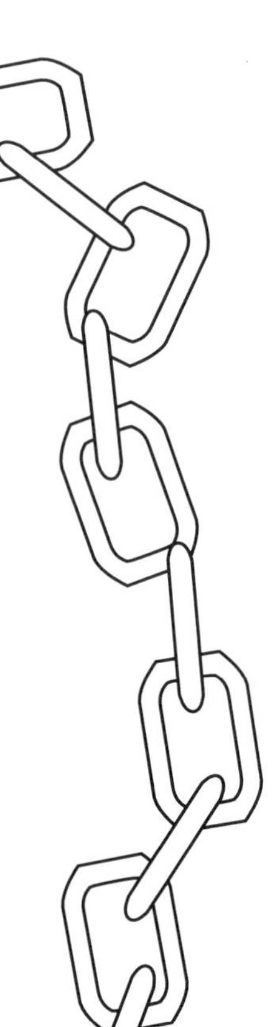

CHAPTER ONE

First Link

The Weapons Factory

The events of my life were about to take yet another significant turn.

It was October or November of 1941, soon after we were required to wear the dreadful yellow star, that I was transferred to a different work site under a new employer. After about two months of working on his road construction job, the owner of the company asked to speak to me. He took me aside and explained that he was in urgent need of a helper for his roofing division.

"The man that runs the tar heater has fallen ill," he explained. "You would seem to be able to handle that kind of a job. I'll pick you up tomorrow morning at 6:00. Oh, by the way," he continued, "don't wear that Jewish star. I am not allowed to bring any Jews into that compound, but I really don't think you look very Jewish. It will be easy to get you in."

As I climbed into the cab of his small panel truck the next morning I was not too sure that going with him was the smartest thing for me to do, but at this point, I had very little choice in the matter. However fleetingly, I reminded myself of the dangers of not wearing that ghastly yellow star. I thought for a moment of the people who had chosen not to wear the star, who were identified and taken away by the Gestapo which by now, had the customary result of never being seen again.

I quickly pushed these nagging thoughts aside when my boss explained as he drove, "The complex we will be working at is a top-secret military operation. Even I am not exactly sure about their product. I was told that they are involved in the manufacture of carbines and handguns. By the way, when we arrive at the guardhouse, I want you to say nothing. These guards have known me for a long time. You will see, they will motion us right through the gate."

The level of my uneasiness and my doubts began to rise again as we neared the compound. A Jew in the middle of a secret Nazi installation! At the same time, in spite of my trepidation, I felt a tingle of adventure.

Engaged with my thoughts, I hardly noticed that my boss had stopped by the guarded gate. With some amount of anxiety I screened the area beyond the gate. I noticed some fairly steep declining driveways. They seemed to lead toward entrances of underground structures.

Just as he had assured me, the guards greeted my boss like an old friend and waved us through, hardly acknowledging my presence. We drove past these driveways and were soon in the midst of several, above-the-ground small two-story, industrial-type buildings. They stood in a heavily wooded area.

The trees were known as *Kiefern.* These are native, very tall, long-needled pine trees with bare trunks and large spread-out crowns. These crowns provide a canopy-like cover above the structures, thus creating an excellent camouflage, making it almost impossible for the not very large buildings to be detected from the air.

We stopped in front of one of the buildings where the roofing job was already in progress. My orders were to heat a large kettle of tar with the firewood that was stacked close by. It did not take long for the rock-hard tar to begin to melt. When it was hot and flowing I filled up one of the old banged-up pails and carried it up the ladder onto the roof. The roofers were a demanding bunch. They yelled if I was too slow or the tar was not hot enough. Surely, I thought, one or two extra logs thrown into the fire hole under the cauldron would keep the tar from getting sluggish while I struggled up the ladder with yet another bucketful of that stinking, scalding pitch.

Descending the ladder again, I glanced toward the kettle. The tar in the kettle had started to roll and bubble. As I stood there for only a brief helpless moment this highly flammable stuff now began slowly creeping over the rim and down toward the roaring fire hole beneath. My stomach clenched with fear and a wave of cold sweat washed over me as I saw the black tar oozing toward the fire hole. I hurled myself at the flaming opening and, with a metal stoker, I yanked out the two biggest burning logs as the flames started to leap upward toward the by now churning tar in the uncovered kettle.

My mind racing, I darted to the plant's fire station, which I had noticed when entering the compound. It was, fortunately, only about fifty yards away, so that in a short time a hastily dispatched small fire engine was extinguishing the tall flames now burning wildly above and around the kettle. The fireman never asked me for my name. Ironically, he even complimented me on my deed and thanked me for my fast action and alertness. He never knew that he was talking to a Jew.

Surely, without my quick response the boiling tar could have become a fiery and explosive flowing mass. Its lava-like surging flow may well have set the surrounding buildings on fire. I shudder when I think of the consequences this mishap could have held for me. A few suspicious questions might have revealed my identity, leading to the incorrect conclusion that I was a spy intent on sabotaging this important secret military plant.

I never finished my first and only day's work as a roofing tar heater. My budding career as a professional tar kettle attendant was now put in serious jeopardy.

The boss drove me home in silence. I suspected that he probably was in shock. He must have recognized how close he came to endangering his own survival. He could have easily been accused of participating in an act of sabotage by bringing a Jew into a secret Nazi military installation.

This close encounter was my first real life-threatening situation since the Nazi system came to be. It is therefore the perfect link in the number one spot in my life's chain of survival.

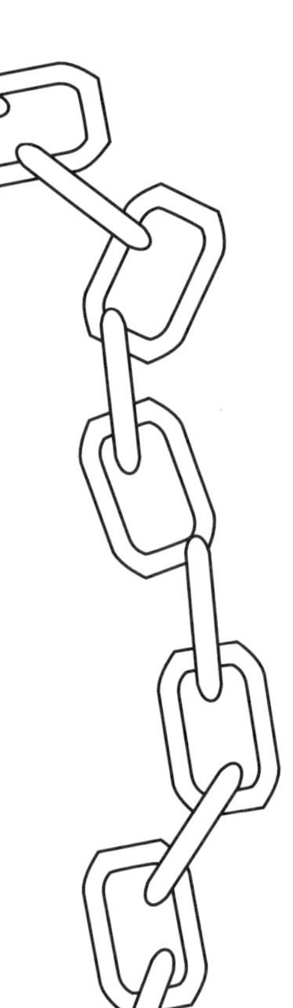

CHAPTER TWO

Second Link

Herr Kaspar the Foreman

By the end of August 1942, Hitler's war had almost completed its third year. He had by now succeeded in occupying several countries of Europe and parts of North Africa. His military steamroller seemed to be practically unstoppable in its devastating momentum as the Nazi troops continued their deep penetration into the Soviet Union.

The massive expansions at the fighting fronts resulted in heavy German losses. In order to replenish the thinned-out front lines, it became necessary to withdraw every reasonably healthy man from the various industries of Germany. Even jails and prisons were affected by the dire need for soldiers. Prisoners of such institutions were taken out of their cells and transferred to concentration camps, allowing the wardens and prison guards to join the military machine.

The shortage of skilled labor became so acute that the Nazi authorities decided to explore the availability of all kinds of skilled workers, even among the Jewish forced labor ranks. The screening of all records apparently revealed the four-year apprenticeship that I had completed to become a designer and builder of fine furniture. Therefore, I was ordered to leave the construction crew and to report to Reinhold's Woodwork Factory in the town of Mariendorf, a suburb of Berlin. I needed to use a commuter train to get there. Since Jews were not allowed to ride on any of the public conveyances, we were issued a special permit that restricted the ride to only getting to the place of work and to return home. It also involved a walk of about fifteen minutes from the station to Reinhold's.

I soon realized that I was totally over-qualified to work there because of the specialized nature of my skills and the fact that Reinhold's busy woodwork factory produced only barracks and related accessories for the military. Nevertheless, I was relieved that I no longer had to work at the construction sites. At the same time, I was thankful that I still belonged to the small number of the remaining Jewish population that had not yet been sent away to a concentration camp. With a group of about fifteen Jewish men, I worked mainly in a separate area of a huge workshop. Herr Kaspar, our foreman, supervised us. (We always referred to him as "Herr [Mr.] Kaspar" because it was inappropriate to address a superior by his first name.) I remember him as a balding, short, middle-aged man. He always wore a tan, tightly buttoned smock that accentuated his slightly protruding belly. We were not exactly crazy about him. He did not treat us badly, but barked his instructions at us in such a way that left no doubt in our minds that he was not too enchanted with us, either. Pinned onto the left lapel of his smock he wore a round, official-looking button that loudly exhibited the wretched Nazi emblem, the swastika, encircled in its center. Whoever wore such a button did it as an obvious attempt to visually document his or her active and loyal membership in the Nazi Party.

He greeted everyone (with the welcome exception of our

group) with a very hearty *Heil Hitler*. Up to that point, the acceptable greeting for the beginning of the day was the conventional "good morning." By now, the Nazi salute had become the official greeting, no matter what time of day. Not everyone was comfortable with this coerced salutation. Many people avoided it at least when greeting acquaintances. But it was necessary to adhere to it strictly when addressing a government employee, a policeman, or any other uniformed person. Failure to salute an official or active Nazi in this'proper' fashion was often interpreted as a person's unfaithfulness to the *Führer* (leader), as Hitler wanted to be called. Such an accusation could easily lead to some uncomfortable questioning by the Gestapo.

Our Herr Kaspar was surely that kind of an enthusiastic Nazi . . . or at least that was what we surmised until one morning in late February, 1943. It was the beginning of our workday and we were about ready to start our daily routine. We were standing in our workshop area, waiting for Herr Kaspar to appear and bark out our instructions for the day.

Our waiting this morning was lasting a little longer than usual, when someone in our crew asked suddenly, "Hey, what's happening?"

"Has anyone seen Kaspar this morning? Is he in?"

"Oh yeah, he's in all right. I saw him outside talking with somebody when I arrived."

"Don't worry, you will hear his mellow and tender voice soon enough," somebody mocked.

It did not take much longer. The door flew open and in its frame appeared a flushed and somewhat excited-looking Herr Kaspar. Cautiously, he closed the door behind him.

"Now listen carefully," he said with obvious restraint and urgency. His voice sounded strangely lower and quieter than usual. Pointing his thumb briefly to his right he said, "I suppose all of you know this factory over there, just a couple of blocks away from us?"

We nodded our acknowledgment.

"Then, perhaps you also know that there is a large group of Jews working in that place. I just found out that at this very moment, trucks are parked in front of that building and the SS are busy loading up these Jews. I also was told that these people are going to be transported to a place called Auschwitz. The same source tells me that their next stop will be right here at Reinhold's, with you most likely marked for the same destination. I know that you will have a bit of time until they arrive here because they started their round-up over there only a moment ago. I am urging you to try to make your work area look as if nobody ever worked here. Most important, sweep the floor and do not leave any particles of wood shavings or sawdust behind. Put every tool in the tool cabinets. Don't leave anything lying around! I want the place to look as if nobody has worked in this area. I am sure they will search all parts of the premises when they stop here. When you are finished, get out of here via the emergency exit. Good luck!"

With that, he quickly disappeared through the door.

We were momentarily stunned when he left . . . not even able to respond with a meaningful "Thank you." We had never expected this man to be a caring human being. "Are you sure that this was *our* Herr Kaspar?" somebody wanted to know.

We hurriedly managed to put everything in order. No one had ever worked faster or had things looking neater than we did in those very few precious minutes. That was the least we could do for him. We recognized that he had placed himself in a situation that could carry grave consequences if the Gestapo were to question him. But we also were relieved at that moment and very thankful that Herr Kaspar's heroic help was making it possible for us to circumvent a fateful encounter with the SS trucks.

We decided to leave individually in order to avoid calling unnecessary attention to ourselves. The fear of being detected seemed to turn that fifteen minute walk to the commuter train station into an endless marathon event. In short intervals, each of my associates appeared individually on the ramp of the station. Trying to be as inconspicuous as possible, we each waited for the train to arrive to take us home, standing apart from each other. Ultimately, I saw that everyone was accounted for and had managed to get away without any problems.

After this incident, I did not dare report to the unemployment office, as would have been my lawful duty. I was sure that I would have been questioned about my previous job, which could have created all kinds of problems, not the least for Herr Kaspar. So I just stayed home and felt extremely lucky that no one appeared to be looking for me.

I never saw Herr Kaspar again. The same applied to my coworkers. For them, the desperate and gallant attempt by our foreman, Herr Kaspar, to save their lives resulted merely in a temporary delay from the camps.

Naturally, at that very moment I had no way to completely comprehend the impact this brave Christian man's action had on my survival.When he mentioned "a place called Auschwitz" we were already very much aware of it as a place where horrible things happened. Some of us had a hard time believing some of the stories of murder and gassing of Jews that were clandestinely reported.

As it turned out, his quick action mercifully delayed my eventual arrival at Auschwitz by more than a year. The fact that over two years later, at the point when I regained my freedom, I weighed only 82 pounds makes it absolutely clear that I could not have survived that additional year in Auschwitz. Clearly, Mr. Kaspar represents the second link in the chain of my survival.

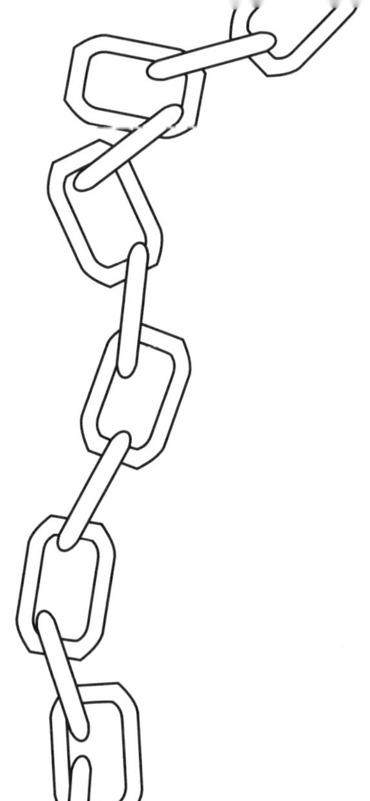

CHAPTER THREE

Third Link

The Visit

By the spring of 1943, Hitler's war had been in progress for about three-and-a-half years. His devastating war machine had succeeded in enslaving most of Europe. By now, about ninety percent of the Jewish population of Germany and Austria had been picked up from their homes or were dragged during sudden, unexpected raids from their work places. Loaded onto trucks, they were transported to and shoved into collection centers where they were held for a few days under cramped and most uncomfortable conditions.

These centers were often synagogues that had been demolished by the Nazis during the infamous pogrom, the *Kristallnacht* of November, 1938. Other places, such as Jewish school buildings had been cleared out and put to use as temporary 'holding-tanks' for the rounded-up victims. Even Jewish old-age homes were made to serve that purpose after the Nazis had callously removed the aged residents and sent them to concentration camps.

The trucks arrived steadily from their round-ups at those locations, spewing out more and more of the unfortunate people. When there was an accumulation large enough to warrant a complete trainload, or transport, as it was termed, the vehicles were loaded again. At the railroad stations the trucks discharged their human cargo onto trains, tragically destined to arrive at one of the dozens of concentration camps located not only throughout Germany but everywhere the Nazis' war boots had trampled.

How would you like to have this "trio" looking for you?

By this time most of the Jewish people that I knew, including members of my family and friends, had been picked up and sent away, 'evacuated' as Hitler preferred to call it. I never heard from any of them again nor did I ever find out to which one of the many camps they might have been sent.

I was still occupying our small apartment in Berlin, together with my mother, Else, and my brother, Kurt. Our mother had been working as a seamstress in a forced labor shop. One day black-uniformed SS troopers suddenly burst into her work area, ordering the Jewish employees out of the building. They pushed them onto the waiting trucks. She and the others were taken to one of these collection centers in Berlin. Of course, at first we had no knowledge of this. When she did not return home from work that evening we feared that something like that must have happened to her. For a few frantic days we had absolutely no idea where she might have been taken.

I knew that a personal inquiry at any of these collection places could have fatal consequences. Merely to approach the guard at the door and ask about our mother would have been tantamount to asking for an invitation to "go in there and look for yourself." Everyone knew that such a move would create a perfect mousetrap. Once inside this building, the only way to get out was via the dreaded truck route. Such action would do nothing but help to add another name to the list of people going away to a concentration camp. Even if I had received permission to enter, I might perhaps only have learned that our mother had been dropped off at a different center. I would have been trapped.

It just so happened that my brother had been ordered to work for a trucking firm. He had previously been a teacher at a Jewish school. When the Nazis commanded the closing of these schools, he had to report to that company, according to the forced labor rules that were established for Jews. This firm was primarily engaged in moving household furnishings during the day. At night, their vehicles were commissioned by the SS to pick up Jews from their premises and, according to instructions from the Gestapo, deliver them to the various collection centers. Without a doubt, this must have been a lucrative assignment.

The owner hardly appeared to be anti-Semitic. He treated my brother and the other Jewish forced labor employees fairly well. However, by accepting this job, this man certainly would not have qualified as an anti-Nazi hero either. Perhaps his theory was, "If I don't pocket all that money, someone else will. It might as well be me."

When my brother told him we feared our mother was in a holding center, he offered to do some inquiring. As it turned out, he had some good connections in the Nazi hierarchy. He succeeded in finding the place our mother had been taken. We desperately hoped that there would be a way to free her.

During this time, it had become necessary for my brother's fiancé, Sonja, to reside with us at our apartment. One day, when she returned to her own home after work, she was horrified to find that her parents had been picked up from their places of work in order to be sent to a concentration camp. Fearing that the Nazis might be looking for her also, we thought it best if she hid in our apartment. The next day, hoping not to be seen by anyone, she returned to her home and was able to pick up some of her personal belongings. Being, in effect, a fugitive now, it was extremely risky for her to leave our home. In spite of the great danger, she tried to collect some additional items a few days later, but had to turn back when she found that the door to her apartment had now been sealed off by Nazi officials.

Just to be on the streets was dangerous for a Jewish person. It was common knowledge that on occasion Jewish people were seized. One had to live in constant fear of a possible encounter with the Gestapo or a confrontation with the regular police. Since the issuance of that decree in September of 1941, Jews were easily identified because of the yellow star they were forced to wear on their outer garments.

Arranging to visit friends was not a simple matter. Jews were not permitted to own telephones, nor were they allowed to use any of the public conveyances. Cars, and eventually even bicycles, were confiscated.

It was quite a blow when I had to give up my bicycle. How would I be able to get around? Berlin was huge and very spread out geographically. A certain date and time allowance was issued during which to deliver the bikes to the nearest police precinct. The Nazis would jump at every opportunity to dehumanize the

Jewish people, so under these circumstances, it was also declared that these bicycles were to be pushed—and not ridden—to their destination. It was not the distance, which in my case was only a walk of about four blocks. It was the very pointed humiliation that resulted. Some Nazis on the street would holler and yell things like, "Hey, look! These Jews are even too stupid to ride a bike!" Others chimed in, "Yeah, why don't you show us!" The situation was very similar when Jews were ordered to give up their pets.

As often as I could, I would visit my girlfriend, Rita. She lived on Prenzlauer Allee, an area of Berlin, known as Prenzlauer Berg. Walking briskly, that long hike from my house to hers took me well over an hour. With full knowledge of all the risks involved, I continued my nearly regular treks to visit Rita. I was young, wanted to lead as normal a life as possible, and was always certain that I would be careful enough to prevent something unfortunate from happening to me.

One day, during a conversation with Kurt and Sonja, I remarked that I had not visited Rita for some time and began making mental preparations for my next journey.

Sonja asked, "Would you mind if I came along with you next time?"

With some concern, Kurt stepped into the conversation. "Sonja, I wonder whether it is a good idea for you to leave here at this moment. As you know, it is wise to avoid the streets . . . it's just too risky!"

A few days went by. Kurt was at work that day. I announced my plan to visit Rita. Because she was in hiding, Sonja had not set foot out of the house for quite some time. She asked how long I intended to stay.

"Oh, not too long," I answered.

"In that case, maybe it would not do any harm if I went along with you."

"Well . . . ," I replied, "I am not so sure. You know that Kurt was not too crazy about that idea when I mentioned it earlier."

"Oh, it will be all right if we just don't stay very long." With that, she readied herself to leave with me.

We walked quickly to reduce our time of vulnerability while on the streets. Finally, we arrived at the large five-story apartment building where Rita lived with her parents and her loveable, elderly aunt.

When we climbed up the stairs and reached their fifth floor apartment we found everybody frightened and in despair. We were told that Rita's father had not returned from work the day before. They had correctly assumed that the SS must have picked him up at his place of work. By now such occurrences were frequent.

For some time we were engaged in somber conversation. I needed to stretch a bit, so I got up from my chair and took a few lazy steps toward the window. I cast a casual glance down toward the street. What I saw made my heart stand still. The scene I observed below me was horrifying! A truck had just pulled up. Four or five SS men emerged and hurriedly disappeared into the big front entrance of our building. There was no doubt about the reason for their arrival: to pick up Rita and her family.

I suddenly recognized the grave danger Sonja was in by being here with me. I knew very well that in such cases, every visitor would be taken along with the family originally intended for the pick-up. We would all wind up on this truck! How could I do this to my brother! Had he not voiced his fearful warnings earlier? Suddenly, I felt terribly guilty for not having tried hard enough to talk Sonja out of accompanying me. How stupid of me! But I also knew that there was no time now to dwell on these thoughts. Quick action was absolutely necessary!

There was no elevator in the house. I knew I had only a few precious moments, just the amount of time it would take the Nazis to come storming up the five stories. I had to think fast! How could I find a way for us to get away? How could I get down the stairs without running into the SS men?

If Sonja had not been with me I probably would have not even considered the possibility of an escape. But her presence certainly determined the urgency of this decision.

Despite their own anxiety, Rita and her mother recognized our horrible dilemma. Urgently directing us to a narrow back door leading to a rear stairway, we said our hasty good-byes. Finding out about that stairway really surprised me. As often as I had been in the apartment, I had never been aware of that rear door. At that instant it became clear to me that it would be impossible to attempt an escape together with Rita and the rest of her family. Rita's mother was pleasant and quiet, but not too assertive. Her aging aunt was fragile and slow moving. I also knew that at this moment the thought of escape would not have entered their minds at all. They were desperate to be reunited with Rita's father, and hoped that this round-up would bring them back together. This way they felt that there would be a chance for them to at least be sent to the same concentration camp. In these situations, to try to stay together with your loved ones was of utmost importance.

It is easy to imagine the scenario if we all had actually tried to escape together. The Nazis' insistent door-banging would have gone unanswered, and in their usual rage and eagerness they would have very quickly forced their way into the apartment, smashing down the door with their big boots. Not finding anyone inside they would have immediately begun storming about, searching the premises with their guns drawn. The back door would have been discovered very quickly and they would have bolted down these stairs, chasing after us. Sonja and I, slowed down by the two older women, would have had no chance at all to escape that way.

Sonja and I seized the opportunity and rushed down the narrow, seemingly never-ending five-story staircase. Having finally reached the bottom floor we found ourselves at a narrow door that opened into a large courtyard. I carefully stuck out my head and saw no one. We darted across the courtyard toward the entrance of a long hallway. Our goal was to make our way through that hallway to the large heavy double-winged door on the other end that would open onto the street.

When we reached that door, in order to determine if the coast was clear, I cautiously pushed against the one wing to open it just a tiny bit. I could barely see through the teeny crack. But that limited view was sufficient enough for my eye to detect a shocking scene. No more than two feet in front of me stood an SS officer, with his back turned halfway toward me. His gun slung over his shoulder, he was guarding the truck and apparently the door. This was obviously not the first time he had experienced people trying to escape. We were trapped! I tried to focus all my energy on our next step. . . !

At the same time, I was suffering intense emotional pain caused by the shocking and unexpected loss of Rita. My heart ached and I realized that there had not been nearly enough time to say a meaningful good-bye. I forced myself to push these feelings aside. I just had to stop and think! This terribly dangerous situation demanded my absolute concentration.

In that dimly lit hallway an idea suddenly struck me. I whispered to Sonja, "I think that we might have a chance."

On the right side, in the middle of the hallway, was the beginning of the long series of stairways, the ones we had previously walked up to reach Rita and her family's apartment. They also were the stairs that the SS men had been charging up noisily. About eight steps up was a vestibule with three entrance doors. Two of these doors were apartment entrances. I pointed to the one in the middle and hurriedly explained that this was the back door of a beauty shop with its main entrance on the street.

Having waited there on occasion for Rita to get her hair done, I was not a complete stranger to the shop owner. Most beauty shops at that time were refusing to accept Jewish customers, but the shop owner and the other beauticians had always treated Rita very nicely. With this in mind, and the likelihood that the Nazis would come down the stairs at any moment with their prisoners, I said to

Sonja, "Quickly, let me go in there. I am sure that they will let us come in and hide."

I was intensely relieved to recognize the owner standing close by as I entered. Somewhat breathlessly I explained our dilemma to her, pointing in the direction of the street where that waiting truck and guard were located and asked her to please allow Sonja and me to hide somewhere in her shop.

"I am sorry," she said, "but if they are really looking for you, they will certainly check every nook and cranny in this building. I just can't risk the consequences I would have to suffer if they found that I was hiding you here." She added firmly, "Please leave."

Frantically, I turned around and hurried out the same way I had come in.

"At least she didn't expose us by forcing me to go through the front door," I remarked to Sonja as I returned to her. "But what are we to do now?"

Feeling desperately trapped we paused for a few precious seconds, hoping for some inspiration. Suddenly, we heard hard boot steps coming from the direction of the courtyard. The sounds came closer and closer, reverberating louder and louder, as they entered the high-ceilinged hallway. Something had to be done quickly! They were so close now, just a few yards away from the stairway platform where we were still standing!

"Come on! Come on!" my mind was racing. In a flash it occurred to me that Sonja and I must have been discovered. Maybe a neighbor had seen us and alerted the Nazis. Perhaps someone had seen us darting across the courtyard.

I whispered to Sonja that it would be useless for us to run up the stairs. They would simply follow us to the very top—to the end of the line. Besides, it was quite probable that at any time now the other Nazis would come down these stairs with Rita and her family.

It suddenly hit me! There was only one other possibility. On the other side of the platform were stairs leading down into a very long corridor of a large, completely dark and musty cellar. In these old Berliner apartment houses every renter had his own partitioned-off, locked-up cellar area along these subterranean gangways. The system was pretty much the same in any building, including the one I lived in. It served as a convenient storage area for potatoes and other vegetables as well as for stockpiling coal and wood for heating. During the air attacks by the Allies, people would seek shelter in their cellar sections. Often there was no electric lighting. People went down the stairs holding candles or flashlights.

Hurriedly, we made our way down the few stairs into the dark, dank cellar, being very careful not to make the slightest noise. Even a whisper could have had fatal consequences. In absolute darkness we carefully felt our way farther along the cold stone wall. Our searching hands suddenly detected a shallow indentation in the wall. It felt just barely large enough for us to squeeze into. We stood with our backs pressed hard into that niche in the wall. Hopefully, that crevice would be deep enough for us to avoid a searching flashlight beam that might be sent down our way.

To our horror, we not only heard, but also actually could feel the threatening reverberations of the Nazis' boot steps as they descended into the cavernous cellar. We were frozen into our positions. They were now talking to each other, complaining about the darkness.

"Boy, is it dark! Do you have a flashlight on you?" I heard one of them ask the other.

"Damn it, no. I thought you had one. Careful now! Let's go in a little deeper. They must be in here!"

They moved closer and closer. Our blood began racing through our veins so loudly, that we were sure it could be heard in the stillness of the cellar. Not more than three feet from where we stood they stopped and listened.

"Do you hear anything?" one of them wanted to know.

Oh God! Frenzied thoughts began shooting through my mind. They were so close! Just one more step and they would find us! My heart was pounding noisily! Panic was beginning to take hold of me! I'd better step out and give myself up, I thought. Maybe that will satisfy them and they won't search any farther.

I had already begun lifting my foot to take the first step, when I heard one of them say, "I don't think anybody is down here."

With that, they turned around and marched away. The relief we felt was indescribable. At the same time, we knew that we could not yet breathe freely. These two SS-men, most likely were still in the building, and their comrades were possibly still upstairs with Rita and her family. We suspected that the sound of their boots would warn us as they came down the stairs. We decided not to move from our spot for another few minutes.

It did not take too much longer. Rita and her family were now coming down the stairway, led by the Nazis. We waited for the retreating sounds of their boots and footsteps to pass. As we heard the heavy front door in the hallway open we also heard the Nazis yelling at their victims, "Move! Move!" A few moments later the revving of the truck's engine reached our ears.

Cautiously, we moved from our hiding place into the hallway. We had to be very careful. A guard could have been left behind. I signaled to Sonja to stay where she was. I moved gingerly toward the exit door at the end of the hallway. Pushing it open slightly, I peered through the slit, saw nothing out of the ordinary and stepped out into the bright, sunlit street.

I was fully aware of the risk I was taking as I spotted the departing vehicle. The still lingering diesel fumes of the truck's engine offended my nostrils. Now, slowly moving, barely fifty yards from me, it was carrying away my dear friends.

At first I feared that a guard on the truck might see me, but since none of them had ever laid eyes on me it was my hope that they would find me just an ordinary citizen out on the street. The back of the otherwise covered vehicle was wide open. On each side of the opening sat a guard, holding his gun upright in front of him. My objective was to just show myself to Rita, her mom and her aunt. I was sure they would look back and see me. Besides hoping for a final glimpse, I wanted my standing there to serve as a signal to them that Sonja and I had been able to escape. I am sure that they saw me from their accelerating vanishing position. As I focused my eyes I was able to see the people on the truck but was unable to distinguish their individual faces.

That was the last time I ever saw them. With my heart aching, I turned around to walk back through the door into the hallway where Sonja was waiting for me.

Fortunately, we arrived home without any further incident. Kurt did not say very much when we told him of our harrowing experience. He recognized how we felt about it. Even though he was saddened for me about my loss, it was obvious and understandable that at that moment the most important matter for him was that Sonja and I had returned home safely.

Suddenly, our mother returned home. It seemed that Kurt's boss had been able to secure her release from the collection center. We experienced a feeling of relief that we were united once again. At least we knew now that if we were picked up, there would be a good chance for us to stay together. At this point we were most thankful that our little family group still consisted of Kurt, our mother, me and of course, the recent addition of Kurt's fiancé, Sonja.

This episode took place during a time when most of the transports were destined for Auschwitz. Once again, the question arises, what would have happened if Sonja and I had been detected and caught by the Nazis? In retrospect the answer is simple enough. In all probability it would have meant suffering additional time in Auschwitz, greatly jeopardizing both of our chances to survive. This link would most likely not have existed and therefore would have eliminated all the ones that follow.

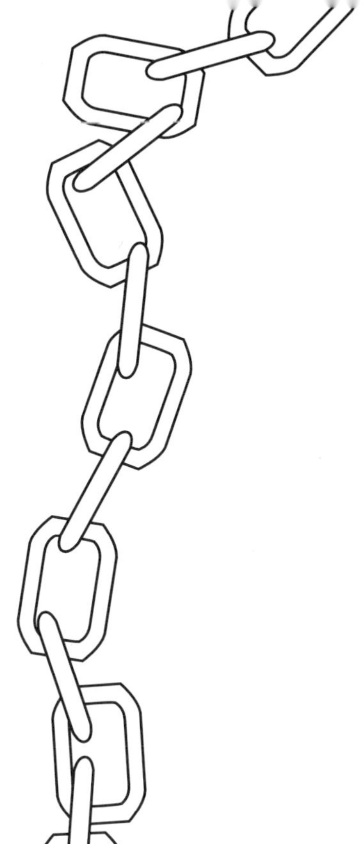

CHAPTER FOUR

Fourth Link

Theresienstadt (Terezin)

Sonja always remained alone when the rest of us were either at work or otherwise out of the apartment. One morning, she was startled when she heard heavy banging on the door. She knew right away that this could not be the knocking of a friend or neighbor. After repeated hammering, the door was smashed down by the Nazis' boots. In a panic, she had just enough time to slide under the bed. From her vantage point she could only see the feet of four men. Four of those eight feet were covered with shiny boots that were obviously part of SS uniforms. The others were clad with regular shoes. After a while, the two uniformed Nazis left, ordering the others to remain until the occupants of this apartment returned. She surmised that it would be impossible for her to hide under the bed for the rest of the day and eventually decided to crawl out. They told her that they would leave now, but that we should be prepared to be picked up by the SS in two days. There was no other place for us to go.

Just about a week before that, I had a foreboding conversation with my loyal Christian friend, Richard Föllmer. As usual, we had to meet under clandestine circumstances, a good distance away from where I lived. I did not want to run the chance of being recognized and, of course, I would never wear the compulsory yellow star on such an occasion. At the same time, Richard was running the high risk of being seen in the strictly forbidden company of a Jew.

He had invited me to have dinner with him at the palatial Hotel Adlon. It was located on Berlin's most famous avenue, Unter Den Linden, right next to the eminent Brandenburg Gate. The by now common sign, warning that Jews were not wanted was prominently displayed near the doorman-guard at the majestic entrance. (The hotel eventually was destroyed by bombings during the war, but was recently rebuilt and reopened.)

We had just put down our wine glasses after making a meaningful toast to better times when I remarked with some hesitancy, "Richard, I just want you to be prepared in case I do not appear at any of our next meetings. I might be picked up by the Nazis." Trying to make my point clear, I added, "There are hardly any Jews left in Berlin. I am almost sure that my turn will come pretty soon."

The whole time I was afraid that eager ears might have been turned in our direction. Richard reacted with great amazement exclaiming, "Oh no, I never gave any thought to that possibility!" But he quickly lowered his voice and leaned toward me as he said, "You had better pack a few things and come to stay with me from now on." I was very moved by his unexpected offer, in particular because I knew that he was fully aware of the risk he was willing to take for himself. I also knew that he lived with his mother in a small apartment. When I thanked him and mentioned that I could not go anywhere without the rest of my family, he even suggested that he would work to find hiding places for all of us.

But time ran out. Two days after the Nazis' break-in, on June

16, 1943, the SS picked up our family. Within a few minutes, allowing only one suitcase per person, the threatening, black-uniformed SS men forced us out of our home. Waiting on the street in front of our building was one of the ominously familiar trucks. Its noisy, smelly diesel engine was running.

We were prodded to quickly climb up into this vehicle. The bumpy ride terminated at one of the collection centers, located at Grosse Hamburger Strasse, a former Jewish school building in the center of Berlin. Coincidentally, it was the one in which our mother had been previously held. Judging by the large number of people assembled inside, it was obvious that the trucks had been very busy collecting and discharging their ill-fated cargo.

After a few days, we found ourselves back on the trucks again. Unloaded at a train station, we were forced into a train whose destination ultimately was the concentration camp of Theresienstadt. It was located in Czechoslovakia, not far from the city of Prague. The Czechs called it Terezin.

To this day, I really do not know what, if anything, 'qualified' us to be sent to this particular concentration camp.The rumor mill had established it as a camp primarily for so-called 'prominent' people. It could have been that my brother, as a teacher, fell into that category. We also considered the possibility that it was due to the influence of the owner of the trucking company for whom my brother had worked. We suspected that it could have been possible for this man to be able to somehow arrange for us to be put on the transport list for Theresienstadt rather than another camp, such as Auschwitz.

It was the Emperor Joseph II of the Austro-Hungarian Empire who built this garrison town, a fortress, in the year of 1780. He named it in honor of his mother, the Empress Maria Theresa. Hence Theresienstadt, "Theresa's Town," *Terezin* in Czech. This fortress was located in the midst of beautiful hilly countryside, in Bohemia.

Under normal circumstances this old fortress could have been the delight of any visiting history professor with his class of eager students. It was completely enclosed by high stone and earthen walls and encircled by a deep, wide moat. It was easy to imagine that it was filled with water at the time of the Emperor's reign and perhaps a long time thereafter. Across this moat, a classic old drawbridge led to the entrance hewn through the huge wall of that forbidding looking enclosure. A network of musty, damp catacombs spread beneath the fortress. For the casual observer it would look just like a scene from a page of a children's storybook. What a perfect setting to fool the world! And to fool the world was exactly what Hitler intended.

The Western Hemisphere began to receive some alarming reports about horrifying atrocities that were taking place in Hitler's concentration camps. At first, in most cases, these reports were discarded as unbelievable rumors. Hitler planned to counter these rumors by trying to create a camp known as a 'resettlement' place for Jews, even though its inhabitants were 'discouraged' from leaving.

Thus, Theresienstadt was developed into a two-faced concentration camp. It was a masterpiece of deception. On the one side it seemed to project an aura of moderate, even happy conditions, exactly the image the Nazis intended to portray to the world in order to counter the "vicious rumors created and spread by World Jewry." Yet, its dominating and horrifying other side was the daily reality of a devastating and deadly system within those walls that had to be kept hidden from the eyes of the world.

This garrison, originally built to house about 7,000 people, would often contain over 50,000 inmates, creating almost choking living conditions. The statistics alone regarding children in Theresienstadt demonstrate the satanic purpose of this place. Records show, of about fifteen thousand children sent to that camp, less than one hundred were alive upon liberation by the Russian forces at the end of the war.

When our group of at least a thousand people arrived, we first were subjected to a sorting-out procedure by the SS guards. They demanded that all jewelry, including wedding and other gold rings, pins, necklaces, earrings, bracelets and watches be turned over immediately. We had to place them into one of the bowl-like containers that were on the tables. They threatened that anyone disobeying that order would get shot. The 'helpful' guards would forcefully and recklessly remove rings from the hands of people who had difficulty getting them off their fingers, often inducing great pain and even injuries. Some women were taken away, ordered to disrobe, and had to submit to the humiliating procedure of being body-searched for hidden jewelry. Our neatly packed suitcases were recklessly ransacked in their frenzied effort to find any other valuable items. As things were found, they were piled up on the table that now displayed several heaps of gold items and jewelry.

After this lengthy and dehumanizing procedure we were all marched away in different directions. My brother and I were assigned a place to 'bed down' in the attic of one of the very large three or four-story buildings that was nearly two hundred years old. It was known as the Hamburger Kaserne (Hamburg Barracks). Before the camp was established, this building, like many others of its kind, had been used as a Czech military barracks. We had to stretch out, side by side, on a wooden, straw-covered floor together with hundreds of other people.

All the dust-ridden structures in this camp were infested with lice, fleas and bedbugs. These unrelenting pests tormented everyone. It was almost impossible to resist the urge to scratch the many terribly annoying, itching, or even painful spots and welts that were all over one's body. The effect was particularly devastating on small children. Their small, dirty fingernails often caused feverish infections. Everyone was painfully aware of the fact that a careless scratch in the midst of such dirty and unsanitary conditions could have grave consequences. That situation alone, aggravated by the almost total lack of medical help or medication, resulted in a great number of deaths among both children and adults.

The scarcity of medical supplies was demonstrated to me when it became necessary for me to seek medical advice. For quite some time I had been bothered by severe pains in my shoulder. The number of Jewish inmates that were doctors and allowed to 'practice' in their makeshift facilities was very limited. In order to see one of them it was necessary for me to stand in line, in the midst of critically sick people, for 3 or 4 hours. When I finally was able to explain my affliction to him he listened very sympathetically, shrugged his shoulders and said: "I do not think it to be anything serious. You are young and the pain will disappear in time. I wish I could give you some aspirin, but I have not seen anything of the sort around for several weeks."

After about two or three weeks on the wooden attic floor, my brother and I were transferred to one of the larger rooms of this old building. About twenty three-tiered bunk beds, with their head ends at the walls, were lined up along each side of the room. The space between the foot ends of the bunks thus created an aisle of about five to six feet in width. It was not exactly luxurious living, but definitely an improvement over the dusty old attic. Lice, fleas and bedbugs feasted on us even here, as if they had moved along with us.

My mother and Sonja were 'housed' in one of the overcrowded rooms of a smaller apartment building that was located on Rathausgasse #2. Often about ten people were squeezed into a smelly room not larger than 15x15 feet.

The narrow streets were constantly packed with people trying to catch a breath of fresh air. Perhaps this air was fresher than that in the living areas, but it certainly was by no means a breath of spring. This ancient and now severely over-crowded place had its very own inherent aroma.

In this camp, adults sent to certain work details could be eligible to receive small amounts of extra food. In the beginning, my brother and I were often placed with such groups. On one occasion we were both assigned to a larger group of men. Every day for a few days, under the watchful eyes of the guards, we were marched out of the camp to a work site about an hour away. Equipped with shovel and pick-ax we had to dig trenches for field irrigation.

We could not believe our eyes when we saw that some of the trenches to be dug would lead right through a large field of huge tomato plants with mouth-watering ripened tomatoes hanging invitingly on their vines. At times we were close enough to snatch and devour a delicious tomato here and there. Of course, being caught in the act would have held very serious consequences for us. Under the steady, watching eyes of the guards it had to be timed just perfectly.

Fruits and vegetables were an unknown commodity in the camp. It seemed only natural that we wanted to find a way to smuggle some of these precious beauties into the camp for our mother and Sonja. As we returned from our work places we were often searched at the camp entrance. Usually, the guards assigned to these jobs were Czech gendarmes, rather than the much more vicious SS guards. Many times they frisked us only lightly, so occasionally we dared take our chances.

It became necessary to resort to some rather strange tomato-smuggling procedures. We would each pull four or five of the smaller ones from the vines and place them next to each other onto a piece of torn-off cloth rag. Now, with the tomatoes rolled up in that rag, a couple of safety pins secured the ends of the rag inside our pants, in front and back, between our legs. Naturally, this required some very gingerly walking! Each successful delivery of these precious items was a moment of triumph for us. During these times of starvation we learned not to be too selective or sensitive when it came to food. Regretfully, the job among the tomato vines did not last very long. However, it created a delicious interlude for us.

The camp's daily menu consisted only of a few simple items. Every day a half loaf of bread was handed out for two people to

Front and back of the ghetto money used in Theresienstadt

share. The greatest care was taken by the two recipients in trying to make the shares as equal as possible, since each gram of bread was important for one's survival.

It was not the easiest task to be fair about. Not only was there no scale, we were not even in possession of a knife. What we did have was a soup spoon made out of soft metal. By hammering the upper part of the handle with a rock, a knife-like edge was created. Either my brother or I would cut this half-loaf lengthwise, thus carefully creating two quarters as equally sized as possible. One of us would then hold both portions behind us and let the other choose. This was by no means for reasons of distrust. It gave us the satisfaction that we did what we could to avoid any, even if only accidentally, created advantage over the other.

In the morning we received only some black liquid, called "coffee." At noon, and in the evening, we lined up outside for a bowl of watery soup. Huge metal barrels, filled nearly to the brim, were wheeled in from the camp kitchen. The grayish-looking liquid actually contained some traces of barley, and here and there a blackish piece of potato or turnip. We soon learned standing too close to the barrel was a thing to avoid. If anyone did, the barrel-attending kitchen helper whose job it was to fill our food bowls often would, with a quick jerk, pull the ladle out of the soup barrel and slam it down on that person's head. The sly grin on the server's face indicated his pleasure, as soup particles splattered all around.

Not very much effort was made to stir up the contents in that barrel. Neither did the 'ladler' care much to dig deeper into the lower area of the barrel that contained the sunken, more substantial food particles. The first people in line therefore received the mostly watery substance from the top. The trick was to try to control any hunger pangs and wait nearby, until the surface of the barrel's contents had reached the more substantial lower level.

It often happened that just as one thought that it was the right time to get in line to receive the thicker part of the soup, the server behind that barrel would almost gleefully stop ladling and switch to the next full barrel. Now, being almost next in the receiving line, one was not allowed to leave and would wind up with the thin soup that had hardly any caloric value at all.

Even with the paltry additional work-related extra rations, it was easily seen that little by little we were losing weight. Old people and others who were unable to work had no opportunity whatsoever to take advantage of the small extra food handouts that were available to some working people. Sadly, looking emaciated, with their clothing hanging from their bony frames, they would always stand near the soup barrels, holding their empty food bowls in front of them.

It was obvious that many of them had come from a very cultured background, but the process of starvation, humiliation, and dehumanization had forced them to become desperate beggars.With their heads lowered they approached us, who were nothing more than their "co-prisoners," in a most humble way, and addressed us with, "Sir, do you intend to make use of your soup?" It was not unusual to find some of these desperately hungry people, their arms having disappeared up to their pits in the garbage bins, scrounging for any food items which may have been discarded from the kitchen. Any piece of food, however dirty or rotten, would eagerly find its way into their mouths. Scenes such as these were certainly not meant to be part of Hitler's intended "revelation" to the world.

At times, instead of the soup we would receive a very tasty, fluffy white baked creation, called a *buchtel.* As it was baking, the delectable aroma coming from the big camp kitchen would waft enticingly throughout the whole camp, creating intense cravings in our starving, empty stomachs. This square-shaped baked item, approximately the size of a hamburger bun, was served with a tasty chocolate sauce, dished out with a tiny ladle not much larger than a thimble. It was absolutely delicious.

I suspected that this spongy food item could not have offered our bodies much of any nourishment. Having wanted to do so for a long time, I finally placed that piece of pastry into the palm of my hand and squeezed it. The result of my experiment left me with a piece of dough approximately the size of a large marble. The offer of such enticing food items was undoubtedly an intentional design to be nothing more than a cruel teaser of satanic dimensions.

I had let it be known that I was trained to design and build fine furniture. Soon after, I was assigned to a workshop that was involved in constructing furniture most likely intended for the camp commander or his staff members. A good amount of furniture repair was also part of the daily workload. Eventually, through my request for a helper, my brother was able to join me. As a teacher, cantor and linguist, he did not have the necessary skills to actually qualify him for this particular kind of work, but somehow we managed to get away with it.

As an act of contemptuous ridiculing, the Nazis issued paper money that was handed out to working inmates. Next to the printed Kronen value was the picture of Moses holding the tablets with the Ten Commandments. The other side showed the signature of the "leading Elder of the Jews of Theresienstadt," Jacob Edelstein. They called it *Ghetto-Geld* (Ghetto Money). Outside the camp it would not have had any more value than the bills of a Monopoly game. Inside, its value was hardly any greater. There were no food stores. The only way to use this so-called currency was to go to the one store that handled all kinds of useless junk, such as old clothing and worthless trinkets that had belonged to the deceased.

The incarcerated population consisted of a great number of specially selected intellectuals. Besides rabbis and cantors, one could find many of the distinguished Jewish community leaders of Germany, Austria and Czechoslovakia. A great number of well-known Jewish artists, writers, poets, composers, musicians and performers of all varieties of stage and cinema were found within this camp's huge earthen fortress. At this point it became clear that Theresienstadt must have held the largest concentration of selected talents ever collected anywhere in such a small area. Jewish veterans of the First World War were brought to this supposedly 'milder' concentration camp. A large percentage of the Jewish aged population was also found here.

It was, of course, the seemingly 'lighter' side of the camp that Hitler had planned to present to the world. Therefore, it was made possible for my brother to make use of his professional cantorial skills by helping to organize Friday night services with three other voices and me assisting in the liturgy. Since there was no synagogue, it took place in a makeshift setting, an old, ugly attic area in one of the old houses. Sometimes, we were able to hold these services outside in the courtyards.

Due to the apparently 'loose' atmosphere it was even possible in some instances for people to get married in a ceremony conducted by a rabbi and a cantor. Kurt and his fiancé, Sonja, were able to take advantage of that situation and were married on April 6, 1944. It was most beautiful and, because of the particular circumstances, a very moving and meaningful ceremony. Of course, there was no way to have a party, not even for our limited family.

With the exception of a few 'prominent' captives in the camp, men and women lived separated from each other. So it was not possible for the newlyweds to have their own quarters. After work they would meet occasionally, but in this over-crowded area of mass confinement it was pretty much impossible to be alone.

During the nearly three years of its existence it happened that several carefully selected delegations received permission to visit the camp of Theresienstadt. The first group came from the International Red Cross. Somewhat later, after Hitler had occupied the small country of Denmark, a Danish delegation visited the 500 Jewish Danish subjects that had been imprisoned in this camp. For some tragic reason, they had not taken part in the dramatic lifesaving operation that had been arranged earlier between Sweden and Denmark, which ultimately resulted in saving seven thousand Danish Jews from being sent to the concentration camps.

Of course, it was always a strictly 'guided tour' along a well-prepared route that was conducted for these visitors. Inmates were instructed to attractively decorate the streets. Boxes with blooming flowers were placed on many of the windowsills for that purpose.

The night before the arrival of the delegations, a small, neat-looking barrack-like structure was assembled and erected in the middle of an expansive lawn that was part of an area called the "Market Place" in front of a big old unused church. That small structure had been previously dismantled and stored away, but was readily available for exactly such an occasion. Shiny white lacquer covered its outside surfaces, and the gleaming red roof with its matching window shutters provided a striking accent. What a beautiful kindergarten structure!

It 'just happened' to be lunchtime as the visiting dignitaries strolled by. The members of the delegation were allowed to come close enough to notice the 'teachers,' in their spotless white uniforms, dishing out delicious food for the youngsters. For dessert, the children were served chocolate. They were encouraged to ask for and actually received second helpings.

The visitors' eyes were now drawn to a small French coffee-house nearby. There, sitting outside on dainty wrought iron chairs placed in front of delicate wrought iron tables, were some carefully selected elderly people being served pastries with hot chocolate or coffee. Cleverly, deceitfully, the Danish delegates were led by their Nazi guides through this area. The Danish visitors, hemmed in by their Nazi hosts were allowed to converse with some of their countrymen. But to speak openly was impossible. The Danish prisoners were fully aware that there were Danish-speaking SS men planted among this seemingly amicable group of Nazi hosts.

Soon after the delegation left that charming French scene, the dainty wrought iron tables and chairs disappeared, and the flowers were removed. The beautiful kindergarten structure was dismantled and returned for storage in the old warehouse, neatly tucked away to assist in deceiving the world again in the future. The children and the elderly people who had unknowingly helped to stage the scenes were sent back to their miserable surroundings. The Red Cross delegations, as well as the Danish one returned home to report that "things were not all that bad," even though they had learned that the people there really were prisoners and were not allowed to leave the premises.

The Nazi propaganda machine, taking full advantage of these statements, announced that 'while the Jews were having chocolates, coffee and cake, the German soldiers were bleeding to death in their desperate fight against the enemy.' Thus, it seemed that Hitler had succeeded in showing the world that the rumors about the camps were "greatly unfounded."

The Nazi propaganda machine fooled even us as they took well-planned advantage of the many talented prisoners to produce the ultimate cloak of deception for the outside world. It appeared that the camp commanders not only tolerated all kinds of cultural, artistic performances, they encouraged such activities. With the overwhelming abundance of performers and artists, many wonderful first-class concerts, stage and variety programs took place on an ongoing basis. At the time, many of us translated that into a glimmer of hope that maybe better things were in store for us.

My brother and I, both blessed with good singing voices, were able to join a huge choir that was rehearsing to perform Haydn's beautiful oratorio, *The Creation.* To have the opportunity to be involved in such creative activity, even after a long day of hard work, was a wonderful way for us to momentarily forget the miseries that surrounded us. The rehearsals often lasted into the late evening hours. Because there was a curfew, it felt good to be given a special permit, which enabled us to walk to our quarters through the now deserted, narrow, nighttime streets.

As performers, occasionally we would receive a small additional item of food such as a tiny little can of chopped liver. But these special privileges paled to the greatest privilege of all: Our conductor, Karel Fischer, announced that he had received a guarantee from the Nazi officials that those of us involved in these rehearsals would be protected from being transported out of the camp. This was of major significance because from time to time people were rounded up and deported to other concentration camps. We had suspected that, however challenging it was to survive here, it would be even more difficult in any other camp.

With this Nazi promise we felt somewhat protected. But in spite of this, it occasionally happened that one of the singers would be missing from rehearsal. We usually found out that this person had been picked up and put onto a train to be part of the fairly regular transports moving out of Theresienstadt. Even so, the deadline for a performance was really never jeopardized. The vast pool of available artists readily yielded a most capable replacement every time. A variety of many wonderful musical and non-musical presentations would also often take place in courtyards and attic rooms. Some of the larger performances were conducted in a rarely used auditorium, called the *Sokolovna.*

The Creation was presented twice. One of the performances featured Kurt as one of the soloists, doing, as always, a superb job.Thereafter we started to rehearse for Mendelssohn's masterful oratorio, *Elijah.* We thought this to be very odd. During the Nazi time no work created by a Jew was permitted to be presented anywhere in German controlled areas. Even though Mendelssohn was a baptized Lutheran, according to Hitler's declaration of the *Nüremberg Racial Laws,* Mendelssohn was still considered a Jew. These laws were not based on a person's religion, but strictly, on his or her 'race,' defined by parents and grandparents.

We also wondered why we were allowed to perform this particular part of a biblical story. Did the Nazis not recognize that this masterpiece of Mendelssohn's was extremely applicable to our situation? Did they not realize that it depicted the great despair of a people under terrible duress and that this duress was most dramatically emphasized as the huge choir cried out the first words of Mendelssohn's masterpiece?

Finally the performance took place. Through an opening in the stage curtains we could observe the Jewish dignitaries walking in and taking their seats. We thought it was odd that the SS staff, outfitted in their fancy dress uniforms, would place themselves next to the Jewish leading Elders for whom they normally showed nothing but utmost contempt. The house slowly filled with people, the inmates of the camp. They had been ordered to dress as well as possible. We, the choir, were assembled on stage behind the curtain and our excitement began to rise. It had never happened before that the Nazis had attended a performance. We thought that this surely must be a special occasion.

At last the curtain opened. Karel Fischer, our dynamic conductor, raised his baton. The music approached the point of the choir's highly dramatic entrance. With the impressive strength of a fortissimo the concert hall reverberated from the combined sounds of the music and the powerfully sung words of the accusing prayer,

"Help Lord—Help Lord! Wilt thou quite destroy us?"

Unquestionably, every one of us in the large choir hurled these words toward heaven and our audience, fueled so amply by all the longing and extreme pain that we had been feeling in our hearts for so long. There is absolutely no doubt in my mind that it would have been impossible for this part of the oratorio to be performed with more meaning and genuine expression—anywhere, anytime.

A second performance was scheduled for about two weeks later. It never took place. A few days thereafter, my brother and I received the order to be at the train station the next morning. It was announced that a transport would be put together in order to send needed workers to a labor camp. Which one or where it would be was left to our own guesswork.

That morning, together with most of the choir members, we

found ourselves among approximately two to three thousand prisoners lining up in front of a long train. It was composed of countless railroad cars, so many that we could see neither the beginning nor end of it. The doors were swung open.

"Schneller, schneller!" We heard the guards' shrieking shouts as we approached the train. Everyone was forced inside—gun butts and sticks striking those who were not fast enough to satisfy the guards and their helpers. We all pushed and shoved into the train in order to escape the merciless and potentially bone-shattering blows. Everybody was cognizant of the fact that a broken bone could cause disabilities, possibly rendering a prisoner useless for work and therefore mark him for destruction.

The doors were slammed shut and securely locked from the outside. Confined now in this mercilessly over-crowded railroad car, I thought of the painful scene when we said good-bye to our mother and Kurt's wife, Sonja, the night before our transport out of the camp. The one thing that was most feared by all family groups, separation from their still surviving members, had finally struck us also. It was always one of the most important considerations, to try to keep the family together, even if it was not always possible to visit freely. Just to know we were in close proximity was of great comfort. Our mother would now be deprived of the comforting thought that her sons were nearby, while Sonja had similar concerns regarding her husband. In spite of our hopeful and encouraging farewell words, our well-concealed trepidation over the uncertainty, if and when we would see each other again, was surely on all our minds. Yet, we were thankful that at least we had had enough warning to be able to wish one another farewell, and that our mother and Sonja still remained together.

I was jolted out of my reflections by the sudden lurch of our wagon. The wheels of the train started rolling, beginning their grinding, clacking, noisy monotonous rhythm. Except for the fact that it had been announced that we would be sent to a labor camp somewhere in Germany we had no idea what our destination would be.

There is no question in my mind that my stay of fifteen months in the camp of Theresienstadt qualifies as an important link in the unbroken chain of the struggle for my survival. Even though I was surrounded by starvation, filth, misery and dying people, subsequent experiences made it clear, that if I had spent these fifteen months in other concentration camps my survival would have been much more doubtful.

From November, 1941 to May, 1945, of the 140,000 people that had been sent to Theresienstadt, 33,000 died of starvation and diseases in the camp. 87,000 were sent on to Auschwitz and other concentration camps to be killed. Of the 15,000 children that entered Theresienstadt, less than one hundred survived.

Hitler's Deceptive Film

It was many years after my arrival in the United States before I learned that Hitler had ordered the production of a film about Theresienstadt. It had been given the ominous title, *Der Führer Schenkt den Juden eine Stadt* (Hitler Presents a City to the Jews). His sole purpose was to focus on 'favorable' images from within the camp, expecting that by presenting this to a suspicious world, he could clear up the 'misunderstandings' about concentration camps.

Painstaking care was taken to avoid any references to the misery and anguish that was suffered by the vast majority of people who had to live under subhuman conditions in this camp. Parts of the footage had actually been produced outside the camp walls, leaving the viewer with the impression that it had been photographed from within the camp.

Clearly, most of the inmates of Theresienstadt had not been aware that a film project was occurring. My brother and I are of the opinion that the only people that were informed, were those immediately involved, like the inmates who were "employed" at the office of *"Freiheitgestaltung"* (Leisuretime creation). This group of people was made responsible for the whole program-of entertainment that was going on in the camp, and therefore also had to be involved in the preparation and execution of such a project. My brother remembers that at one time he heard a rumor about some kind of filming, but neither he nor I actually witnessed any of it. Yet, a fragment of this film shows us standing in the tenor section of the choir. But to this day we cannot figure out how the *Elijah* was filmed without our noticing it.

I was in the States many years when I learned that some surviving fragments of this partially destroyed film had been found by the Allies. At that point I had no way of knowing whether or not parts of our *Elijah* performance were filmed. But the thought later occurred to me that if it was, this was perhaps the reason the originally scheduled second performance was forfeited. Apparently there was no need for 'a second take' since the first rendition must have proven to be acceptable. The cast was not needed any longer, and could now easily be disposed of and loaded onto the train to be sent away.

For some reason I did not think that this film could be available, therefore I never bothered to pursue the matter any further.In November of 1995, as part of the of the "50th End of World War II Commemoration," Nick Strimple, a musicologist from Los Angeles presented a lecture in Minneapolis, Minnesota about music in the concentration camp of Theresienstadt. I had family and friends in my car. The parking lot was loaded. I let everybody out of the car and went to find a parking spot somewhere on the street. It was rather difficult and a bit time-consuming. I walked in a little late, thus missing a few minutes of his presentation. The very moment I entered the auditorium I caught a glimpse of a just disappearing slide pictured on the screen. I could have sworn that the brief image that lingered on in my mind was that of a section of our choir in Theresienstadt during the performance of the *Elijah*. Not only that, I thought that I had even recognized my brother and me in that short moment on the screen. When I talked to the lecturer at the end of his delivery he informed me that this was a picture taken of a scene from a Nazi-propaganda film. He graciously offered to send me some still copies of these scenes, which arrived soon after and proved my impression to be correct. Yet, since the pictures were not perfect (they were taken from damaged film) I wanted to see it on the film track itself to be absolutely sure.

It took two or three months for me to hunt down and acquire a copy of the surviving fragmentary clips of this vicious Nazi product. Sure enough, it presents a very small segment of the performance of Mendelssohn's *Elijah.* The musical score of this fraction is not in perfect condition, yet it is easily identifiable. To my great astonishment, I discovered that my brother and I were actually visible, standing next to one another in the tenor section of the choir, (Unbelievable!) Karel Fischer, our conductor, standing right in front of us.

(It is my understanding that he did not survive.)

Henry and his brother, Kurt, are in this choir which performed Mendelssohn's "Elijah" in Theresienstadt for Nazi dignitaries. A few days after, many of the singers were shipped to Auschwitz.

CHAPTER FIVE

Fifth Link

Late Incarceration

After I had my first chance to witness life in a concentration camp it occurred to me that it was a most fortunate circumstance that my family and I had not been picked up before June, 1943, a comparatively late date. By then about ninety percent of the Jewish population of Germany and the Nazi occupied countries seemed to have simply vanished.

Up to about two years before this time, some of the wealthier members of the Jewish community had been able to immigrate to countries that had opened their doors. These tended to be people with large financial backing. Our widowed mother, my brother and I did not fall into that category, so we were in no position to have been considered by any of those countries.

The only other opportunity for us would have been to find a relative or close friend in the USA who would be able and willing to issue an affidavit of support. In anticipation of such a miracle, or just to take advantage of any other chance that might possibly develop we registered at the American consulate. Now, at least, we had a number on the waiting list of their very limited immigration quota.

My mother eventually remembered a distant relative in New York and wrote to him. She had reason to believe that he would be good enough to rescue us by providing the precious affidavit. She wrote to him, explaining our desperate situation. He immediately informed us that he would be glad to attend to the matter right away.

"All you have to do is to wait for the confirmation by the American consulate," he wrote. Several months went by. Finally the so eagerly awaited invitation to come to the American consulate arrived. We were so elated that we practically started packing!

When we arrived at the consulate we found ourselves among a throng of other desperate people who had converged in front of the building that represented the gate to all of our freedom. After hours of waiting we finally were escorted into the consul's office. He was so nice! After offering us a cup of coffee he opened the file that was lying before him on his desk. We nervously watched as he flipped through a few pages, thoughtfully studying them.

We anxiously waited, suppressing the urge to say, "Come on already! Give us the date of our visa!"After what seemed to us an eternity he finally remarked, "I am very sorry, but it seems that this affidavit is financially lacking. It will be necessary for you to ask your sponsor to find a way to increase its value."

What a devastating disappointment! Our mother informed our relative immediately. He could not understand it. He thought that he had more than satisfied the requirements, but promised to make sure that it would be taken care of immediately. We are sure he tried. But before we could receive any good news, the consulate was closed. Our situation, obviously, had not been considered an emergency.

Until that fateful day of June 16, 1943, we had been hoping we would be spared being picked up. Our conviction was that we could manage to survive until the certain and—what we believed—very near victory of the Allied Forces became a reality. While the Nazis never officially admitted any of their military setbacks there were people listening secretly to prohibited radio stations, like BBC and others. As a result of that, somehow, word got around when the Allied Forces were successful in repelling and reversing some of the German military advances.

As miserable as our living conditions were, with all the choking restrictions, we had no doubt at all that the conditions in a concentration camp would be much, much worse. The first round-ups of Jews had already taken place almost five years prior to ours.

Looking back now, and considering my very poor physical condition at the later part of my incarceration, it is absolutely clear to me today that I could not have endured being confined at any earlier period. Spending additional time in any of the concentration camps most certainly would have meant my demise.

Thus, our late incarceration became a link of my survival.

Sixth Link

Brothers Not Separated

In most cases, at one time or another, the Nazi guards routinely separated family members in order to promote a sense of fear, isolation and dehumanization. The inhumane separation of loved ones was a technique often ruthlessly applied and was one of our greatest fears. So far we had been fortunate enough not to be split up and we hoped this situation would remain.

Our staying together not only enabled us to monitor each other's moods and well being, but to provide consolation and support as we needed it. Our strong family ties bolstered our will to survive. Occasionally, the strength of this 'will' would be particularly challenged and we would each take turns at becoming discouraged and blue. By talking to each other we were able to overcome our sometimes depressing moods. One or the other of us would quickly express some optimistic and positive thoughts, such as:

"After all, we are still in comparatively good condition."

"We are still in good enough shape to be utilized for work."

"Just look around you! All in all, we are still pretty lucky. It could be a lot worse."

"The Allied Forces are beating the Nazis left and right."

"Just sit tight, it won't be very long until we are freed."

My brother and I had always been blessed with a good sense of humor. Even under our miserable circumstances there were some situations that, at least to us, appeared to have a somewhat comical side, causing us to utter an inappropriate comment or two. That was, of course, only after we made sure that any guards within earshot would not accidentally 'benefit' from our sarcastic remarks and that the remarks would not get us in trouble. (For some understandable reason, we did not have too much confidence in their senses of humor!)

Sharing humor not only kept us from focusing on our desperate condition for a few brief moments, but it was also gratifying to see the effect on some of the otherwise drawn faces all around us. At times, it even encouraged someone else nearby to make a terse remark that would inspire a not-too-common smile to last a little while longer. There was no doubt in my mind that humor gave us strength, and proved to be a great anesthetic.

As time dragged on, trying to survive in the camps caused everyone to become tired and listless. Each individual became increasingly involved with his or her own survival, and as everyone's strength was waning it became very unrealistic to expect any support from others. Kurt and I were always very close and had every intention not to let anything change that situation.

So, the fact that we were able to avoid separation, definitely, is another important link in the chain of our survival.

CHAPTER SIX

Auschwitz/Birkenau

The train wheels ground to a screeching halt.

Just about an hour before, someone nearby in our miserable confinement spoke up. "I think I have bad news. I am pretty familiar with this countryside." With alarm in his voice he added, "I am quite sure that we are not very far from Auschwitz!"

"You must be mistaken!"

Somebody replied with disbelief, "Auschwitz is not a labor camp! We were led to understand that we would be sent to a labor camp!" We all knew from what we had heard that this, of all the camps, was the one considered to be the most dangerous. Horrible stories about Auschwitz abounded. "He has to be wrong or confused" we mumbled to each other, "so many countrysides look alike."

We had rolled out of Theresienstadt to begin an experience that proved to be even more terrifying than I could ever have imagined. It was the beginning of October, 1944, but time seemed to have come to a standstill as we waited for the heavy doors to be unlocked and finally opened. The old, coughing steam locomotive, with its endless chain of cars in tow, had finally stopped at the train ramp of the infamous extermination camp, Auschwitz/Birkenau.

Confined in one of these old railroad cars, we had just survived a horrifying two-day ride. Many of us had not even had the chance to have a seat on one of the hard, wooden slat-constructed benches on which people sat squeezed uncomfortably close to each other. Some of us were in a crouchposition on the dirty floor between those benches, cramped in so tightly that there was hardly enough space to move our arms. Others were sitting on the stacked up suitcases that were crammed together with us into the train. The almost steady squirming of the people around us made it practically impossible to fall asleep. Yet in some cases, sheer exhaustion helped us ignore the discomfort and allowed some people to doze off for awhile.

We were part of a group of men ranging from the very young to the very old, from the fairly healthy to the hopelessly frail, emaciated and seriously ill.

Every car had a toilet, but making use of it was almost an impossible task. The over-crowding prevented the intended facility-users from getting there, and the many sick prisoners, as well as the over-usage of the facility, caused it to be a most sickening and revolting scene.

Although the train had stopped often for hours, we had never been given the opportunity to set foot outside where we could have stretched our cramped bodies for a while. Many were too sick and weak to survive this cruel ride and died even before arriving at Auschwitz. Their lifeless bodies had to remain in the railroad car because the doors were never opened. There was no way to dispose of them. During all of this traveling time we never received a drop of water or a piece of bread.

And yet, listening later to other prisoner's reports it turned out that we could consider ourselves pretty lucky. "We were shoved into cattle cars, 90 to 100 prisoners in each, so tightly that there was no place for anyone to sit down," one of them told me."For a toilet one filthy bucket, soon overrunning with excrement, stood in the corner to be used by everyone in the wagon, men, women, boys or girls. The doors during that nearly three-day ride were never opened. By the time we arrived in Auschwitz about one third of the passengers had died," he exclaimed. "We had no choice but to stack up the bodies at one end of the wagon . . . up to the ceiling, wedging one of them in on top to keep the stack from collapsing." I heard these reports from many other co-prisoners, and later, survivors.

A while after our arrival at the long and seemingly endless train ramp of Auschwitz/Birkenau the heavy doors were finally unlocked and forcefully opened, producing their unmistakable slamming noises. Immediately, the yelling and barking of the SS guards and their helpers put us on high alert to follow their orders and instructions quickly with their always accompanying, *"Schnell! Schnell!"* We were ordered to line up outside in front of the cars. All along the train the survivors of this ghastly ride were staggering out. Many had hardly enough strength to maneuver the high steps, that led down onto the ramp.

Looking up and down the long, endless train, my brother and I found ourselves lined up among the hapless arrivals, comprised of mostly very tired, exhausted and starved people. This long line stretched out as far as our eyes could see. At last we were able to fill our lungs with fresh air!

It took our noses a moment to adjust as we came out of our stuffy and foul confinements.What we inhaled as fresh air was unmistakably laden with the repugnant, yet familiar odor of burnt flesh, a smell reminding us of the crematoriums of Theresienstadt. The tall smokestacks on top of the nearby crematoriums were busily spewing out the product of their waste. Here and there, the tiny white speckles of telltale ash swayed in the air, lingering for a moment before starting their slow descent to the ground. We had heard of people being sent to gas chambers and their bodies subsequently burnt, but our minds at first resisted allowing any concluding thoughts. Anyway, this new situation demanded our total attention.

We stared at the long line of SS guards, placed every few yards from each other. They stood along the opposite side of the ramp, not more than ten yards across from us. They were facing us with their guns slung over their shoulders. Huge ferocious-looking German shepherd dogs accompanied several of them.

Our weak and tired bodies stood on this ramp for quite a while when it was announced that we would receive food once we were inside the camp. We were informed that before this would happen several procedures would have to be carried out, and that it would be in our own best interests to comply with the orders as swiftly as possible. We were advised that the more quickly we acted the sooner we would be taken inside the camp where our food would be waiting for us.

The announcer informed us through a megaphone in a hoarse-sounding voice that everyone would be very much needed for work. Therefore, he even suggested that medical assistance would be provided, and if necessary, a few days of rest to recover strength would be allowed. All those requiring such help needed only step forward into the middle of the ramp.

Many of the people, even some of the younger ones, were in such deplorable physical condition that they could hardly hold themselves upright. As they dragged themselves toward the designated area they hoped and trusted that deep within their oppressors' hearts a glimmer of humanity might have remained. "Could it be possible that this time, they meant what they had promised?"

When quite a large group had finally assembled, they were taken away by the same route the previously sorted-out group of very old people had gone. Our captors had concluded that these people were not worth any costly medical treatments, after all. They would not be able to provide any useful kind of work and

A typical concentration camp barrack for prisoners (Auschwitz) (top). Inside a concentration camp barrack. Prisoners slept in three vertical rows on wooden boards (bottom).

therefore did not qualify to receive the bowl of watery soup and the piece of dry bread. This was simply the end of the line for these people. They were now escorted into the gas chambers, from which their lifeless bodies would be carted finally into the adjoining crematoriums.

Most of us had recognized that any chance for survival depended simply on the ability to report to work. The Nazis were not interested in wasting their time and effort feeding the Jews while nursing them back to health. Being fully aware of this, many people chose to try to conceal their often dire conditions, and did not step forward when medical assistance and resting time was offered.

Up to this point, we had managed to survive Hitler's war for more than five years. As isolated as we were in the camp, from time to time we were able to get some often only fractional information from the outside. It usually was brought into the camp by prisoners who were assigned to work in guards' quarters and were able to either listen to their conversation or hear some announcements on the radio. At this late time in the war even the Nazi command could not keep all their defeats a complete secret.

We heard about some serious setbacks suffered by the Nazi forces and believed that their defeat and surrender was imminent, perhaps just a few weeks away. The consensus was that we just needed to continue to "hang in there," to report for work and wait for the Allied Forces to be victorious. Mercifully, we could not know at this moment that this victory was still quite a few months away from happening.

We were still standing on the ramp without having received any food. The terrifying sorting-out procedures were progressing very slowly. We then were ordered to move forward in single file formation. Our long, long line proceeded ever so slowly toward the end of the ramp, which led into the entrance of the camp. There stood a towering, high-ranking SS officer clad in a spotless snappy uniform. His feet were planted unwaveringly inside his knee-high boots that were polished to a mirror-like lacquer finish.

He was facing us as our long single-file column of people slowly approached him. With an arrogantly critical eye he judged the possible usefulness of each prisoner passing before him. The extended thumbs of his shiny, black kid-leather gloved hands pointed either to the left or to the right. With this completely soundless method he succeeded in heartlessly weeding out the people who were attempting to survive by pretending that they were still well enough to work. One thumb, pointing in one direction, we later found out would condemn a human being to the extermination camp, while the other thumb, pointing in the other direction, would direct the more able-appearing prisoner to enter the site of the concentration camp of Birkenau, the more labor-oriented part of Auschwitz. My brother and I were fortunate that this 'almighty thumb,' reigning over life and death, had directed us into the Birkenau site.

As we were originally instructed, our two suitcases had our names boldly smeared on their fronts in big, white letters. They held whatever remaining possessions we had. We were not allowed to take them with us into the camp and never saw them again.

In front of a large barrack serving as a shower facility, we were ordered to shed all our clothing. The short, soapless but hot, shower was a treat we had not experienced for a long time. We were not given towels as we stepped out, shivering, into the cold October air. Off to the side, was a long line of tables piled high with stacks of striped prisoners' uniforms.

Being restrained from reaching these tables and at the same time most eager to cover our wet, naked bodies, we were ordered to create several single file formations. After a while, some camp inmates appeared with manually operated hair clippers in their hands. They placed themselves in front of each line and began clipping. Our hair was shorn from all over our bodies. Since the clippers were old and missing a tooth here and there, this procedure was not a very pleasant one for us. I think that more hair was jerked out rather than cut off. But due to the intimidating situation and the fact that we were new arrivals, no one dared even whimper.

This was a long procedure. Still naked and feeling quite dehumanized, we were now hoping to be allowed to reach for those hideous blue and white striped uniforms and thus at last be able to cover ourselves. But this was not yet to be the case.

Once again, we were ordered to create and stand in several single files. Another announcement was bellowed out. "From this time forward, you will not be allowed to use your name and you will respond only with the number that will now be assigned to you. Even if a guard were to ask for your names, you will only reply with your assigned number."

The menacing voice continued. "Since there will be no identification cards and any newly-assigned number might easily be forgotten, we think it would be a good idea to tattoo that number right onto the skin of your arms!" The dehumanization process had now reached its pinnacle. We suddenly came to the realization that until now our names had been our very last personal possession. One by one, as we inched our way forward in the line, the tattooer with his busy needle distorted our arms with this wretched number. This all took a very, very long time. Finally, we made our way to the tables and at last received our striped prisoners' clothing.

The material of the underpants I received had a very familiar look about it. I was horrified to recognize that they were made from a most important religious item of the Jewish tradition, a prayer shawl *(tallith).* This shawl is worn as an essential, ceremonial part during the *Shabbat (*Sabbath*)* and holiday services at the synagogue, as well as on other festive, religious occasions. For example, during the celebration of a son becoming a Bar Mitzvah a father usually gave it ceremoniously to his thirteen-year-old. (Today a vast number of congregations equally bestow this ceremony onto their daughters who become Bat Mitzvah. Before World War II this was not customary.)

With rare exceptions, every Jewish man owned a *tallith.* Therefore, it was a fundamental and revered part of his luggage, along with all other important items that he carried with him when he was sent to the camps. After confiscating the luggage the Nazis ordered these holy objects especially to be sorted out and collected, so that they could be sewn into underpants. This action clearly demonstrated their ultimate disrespect and repulsion for anything that was cherished by Jewish people. I felt very sad when I put them on, but I had no choice. It seemed that this formerly cherished item was now deemed to serve an entirely different, but also very important role . . . to help protect us a little from the cold.

These various procedures had taken up most of the day. By now it had turned dark and was late in the evening. When we were finally assigned to the barracks we received a bowl of watery soup and a piece of bread. It felt like a feast after our long period of starvation.

Barrack of Auschwitz/Birkenau

The 'accommodations' were quite different from what we had had in Theresienstadt, where straw-covered bunks served as beds. We certainly had complained about how uncomfortable they were, yet in time, we even had gotten used to them. But here, as we were driven into these barracks the picture was quite different.

All along the walls, extending totally from one end of the barrack to the other there were three, sometimes four tiers of endless shelves, deep enough to serve as a base for sleeping. In some other barracks individual bunk shelves were nailed together in separate units, but were shoved tightly together from one end of the barrack to the other, giving the impression of endless shelving. Each evening after returning from our work details we first had to stand outside the barracks in head-count formation, sometimes for hours on end, with more than a thousand prisoners lined up in front of each one of the barracks. Finally, the order to enter was yelled out. The guards and their helpers ruthlessly enforced these orders with their usual all too familiar gun butts and heavy sticks, accompanied by steady and customary shouting of *"Schneller! Schneller!"* The uncontrollable mad rush, created by this beastly action, resulted in relentless pushing and shoving. Every prisoner was desperately trying to avoid the potentially disabling bone-fracturing beatings. Whoever was first through that door would have to run—not walk—all the way to the other end, climb up to the top tier, and lie down on his back. By that time the next person had been driven in and also had to climb up and stretch out on his back next to the first one. The guards watched intently and shouted, "Touch elbows, touch elbows!"

No space was to be wasted. This went on until the whole length of the top shelf was filled from one end of the barrack to the other. The procedures for filling the two, sometimes three, shelves below were identical. This system made it impossible to occupy the very same place on the bunk every night. There was just nothing one could call one's own. Only one, often soiled, blanket was available for each person.

So far, my brother and I had been fortunate, fast and alert enough to avoid most of the sticks and gun butts. Regretfully, the dull, thudding sounds made by connecting hits were heard only too often. Not everyone, after long incarceration, was fast enough to escape all of the murderous beatings.

The morning wake-up calls came very early. We had to remove the bodies of the prisoners that had died during the night. Nobody had any strength to spare. If the deceased was on the top shelf, for instance, the body was pulled to the edge and just dropped onto the floor. From there, the body was dragged to the outside and piled onto a usually already existing pile of bodies. Another group of prisoners was assigned to load them onto a wagon and drag the macabre load to the crematorium. This was a scene duplicated in every one of the hundreds of barracks in this hellhole.

Returning immediately to my overnight location I had to neatly fold up the blanket that I had used and place it at the foot end of the spot I had occupied during that night.

We were then ordered out of the barrack to assemble in head-count formation. After completing whatever other rather lengthy procedures may have entered their minds, we were marched off to work, often being forced to sing a song in a rhythmic and energetic cadence. Our work here consisted usually of a variety of menial, clean up tasks lasting 10 hours or more. The same routine would be repeated day after day.

Without warning, a few weeks later we were loaded onto trucks and found ourselves on the way to yet another concentration camp.

CHAPTER SEVEN

Seventh Link

Health (Ability to Work)

In every one of the camps, the absolute necessary link to survival was having the strength to be able to join the daily marching column for the purpose of being taken to the work area.

With the exception of my contracting a more serious ailment a few weeks prior to my liberation, I do not recall having been plagued by anything, not even by a cold or the sniffles. I am sure that at one time or other I might have contracted a flu, felt feverish or had another illness, but I learned not to pay attention to it. Every prisoner who wanted to survive, simply joined the marching columns, always disregarding any physical discomfort, no matter how miserable he felt.

It could be that the reason I am not able to recall any bouts with pain, nausea or anything else lies in the fact that I did not pay much attention to any minor problems. It was just our good fortune that during the times when we had to report for work, nothing of a really serious nature struck my brother or me.

I only could hope and pray that my emaciated body would not contract any severe illness. It was also necessary to always be on the alert, avoiding any potentially dangerous situations that could easily result in a beating by the guards' gun butts. The equally deadly sticks and fists of their helpers were just as likely to cause a broken bone or two. Any of these situations would have been tantamount to a death sentence.

Eighth Link

Youth

At the time of my incarceration I was twenty-two years of age. There is just no question that being a young adult in prime physical condition had to be of great value in the desperate fight for survival. Even in the camp of Theresienstadt, very few older people were able to survive the inhumane demands of long hours of hard labor. The ones who were too old, as well as the ones not able to work, just did not have much of a chance at all to survive. The combination of much less than adequate food rations, subhuman living conditions and an almost total lack of health care took its greater toll on most of these unfortunate people from the beginning of their arrival in the camps.

Also, not only at Auschwitz/Birkenau, but in any of the other extermination camps, most of the Jews of advanced age were immediately separated at their arrival and taken away to be destroyed. The same was true of children under 15. Unproductive mouths to feed were unwanted.

Ninth Link

Stature

Astonishing as it seems, being of small stature contributed to my chances of survival. I was five feet-six inches tall and weighed about a hundred and thirty-five pounds. Even though I was not a giant, I was in good physical condition. During my professional training I had been subjected to plenty of strenuous activity. Carrying lumber, lifting heavy furniture, loading and unloading trucks with lumber and furniture was something I had to do on a pretty regular basis. It resulted in helping me to develop a good amount of physical energy. The time I worked at various construction sites during my forced labor jobs was also beneficial in developing strength.

Even so, while I was working alongside other prisoners in various work details in the concentration camps, I could not help but be envious of those men who were much bigger and stronger than I was. Impressed, because they appeared to be able to handle the hard physical chores with much more ease than I, my initial thought was that anyone blessed with such strength would have a much improved chance of survival.

One of the great and ironic tragedies of life in a concentration camp was that just the opposite was the case. These big men were fed the same meager amount of food that the smaller person received. In comparison, it was soon noticeable that their size and strength began to wane at a much faster pace than that of a smaller person.

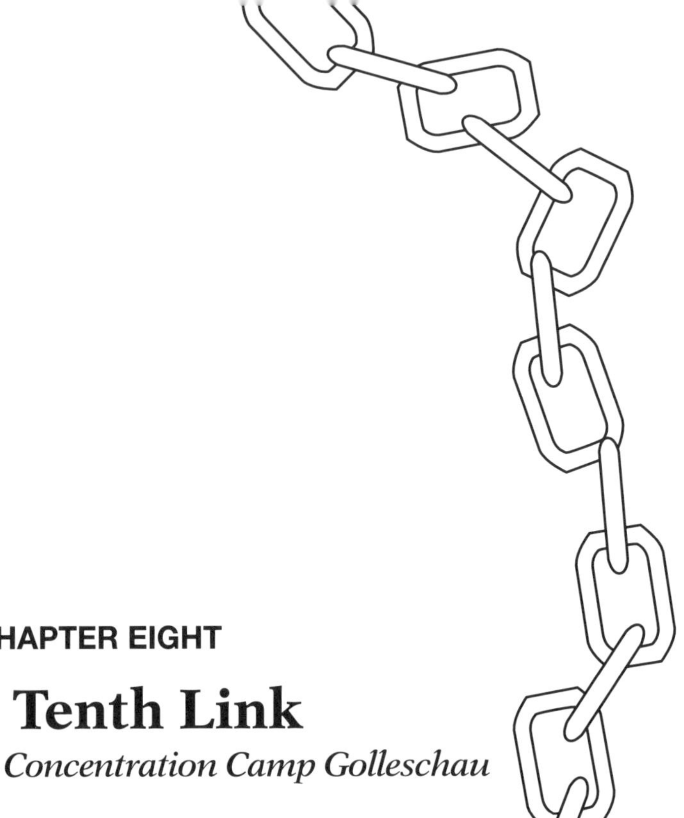

CHAPTER EIGHT

Tenth Link

Concentration Camp Golleschau

Having left Auschwitz/Birkenau, we arrived after a bumpy 20-mile ride on a truck, at a small concentration camp called Golleschau, a satellite-camp of Auschwitz. Golleschau was mainly a large cement factory with its stone quarries located nearby. Having just been ordered off the trucks, and herded by the ever-present SS guards, we awaited our next instructions.

Nothing happened for about an hour, until one of them snarled at us, demanding our attention.

"We are in need of a few people who are experienced in wood-working," he bellowed. "Those who are, step forward. *Schnell! Schnell!*"

This sounded like a job opportunity made right to order for me. I quickly stepped out in front of the group, my body freezing into the always-required position of attention while awaiting further orders. Several other men did the same. We followed the guard to a spot where there was an enormous pile of wooden railroad ties.

He screamed, "They are piled up at the wrong place. I want you to stack them right over here. *Schnell! Schnell!*" He then walked off a distance of about twenty-five yards to indicate the spot where he wanted us to move them.

As we lifted and lugged these heavy wooden monsters, the grinning faces of the guards displayed the pleasure they derived from our obviously humiliating situation. I could not help but feel extremely stupid, embarrassed and angry to have allowed myself to fall for such a cheap trick. When this job was done I felt totally worn out, and I promised myself never to volunteer for anything again.

We suddenly heard from our tormentor once again, "I think they looked much better where they were before! Just get them back there—*Schnell! Schnell!*" The previous incarcerations had unmistakably and visibly left their marks on our bodies. Carrying these railroad ties required a tremendous amount of exertion. We labored very hard for a long time, and were completely exhausted when finally all the ties were piled at the originally designated spot.

We were housed in a huge four-story brick building that formed a rectangular compound, enclosing a sizeable courtyard. A considerable number of prisoners were packed into each of the very large rooms of that complex. But here at least, we did not have to spend the nights on long hard shelves. Rather, inside each room were rows of three-story very narrow bunks that had been thinly covered with straw. There was even the "luxury" of a very small straw-filled sack that served as a pillow.

One evening, my brother told me that he had met a former student of his. This young man had fortunately been chosen by the SS guards to work in their quarters. It seemed that he was able to occasionally smuggle a piece of bread into the camp.

It was the night before my birthday. As a birthday present my brother handed me a piece of life-sustaining bread, part of which he had received from his young friend.

I had intended to celebrate my birthday the next morning by eating the bread for breakfast. Every morning, a bowl of black water, called 'coffee,' was dished out without any food accompaniment. I was looking forward to my festive birthday-morning meal. At bunk time I very carefully hid the piece of bread under my straw pillow. The ruthless wake-up call the following morning made me anxiously anticipate my breakfast feast as I eagerly reached for my birthday present.

How sadly disappointed I was when I could not find it. Someone in the room must have seen me hide it and stolen it while I was asleep. I not only felt dismal for myself, but the thought that my brother had deprived himself of something that he sorely needed for his own survival, made me feel even worse. Why did I not eat it right away? I should have known better! This time I had slipped! I think the anticipation of my birthday breakfast had made me careless.

Theft out of desperation for survival was by no means an uncommon act. During the harsh coldness of wintertime the thin, often rag-like striped jackets of our prisoners' uniforms afforded little protection. So clearly, the extra layer provided by owning two of these items would certainly help protect a little more. Therefore, one always had to watch his jacket carefully; removing it one did not dare let it out of one's hands. There were incidents where hunger pangs were so dominant that a jacket was traded in for a piece of bread.

The prisoners worked primarily in the cement factory and the stone quarries. Once again, I let it be known that I was trained to design and build furniture. After only a few days I was singled out of the morning head count. A guard, without telling me the reason, ordered me to follow him. This was a precarious situation and I knew that a prisoner singled out that way often would not return.

We walked for fifteen minutes during which the guard did not utter a sound. I began to relax as we marched in the direction of a building with a large sign above the entrance, identifying it as a *Faßfabrik* (Barrel Factory). Various sizes and styles of wooden barrels were being produced here predominantly by Polish slave workers, under the menacing eyes of members of the German Nazi-occupation forces.

He took me into a room that was outfitted with a drawing board, a work bench, all the necessary woodworking tools and stacks of different kinds of lumber. Suddenly, he addressed me, speaking in a short, abrupt tone as though it was difficult for him to have to talk to a Jew. He informed me that I was to design and build a large, fancy hand-polished conference desk of solid mahogany wood.

"You will be permitted to use any of the woodworking machines in the factory's machine shop. Just let me know when, and I will escort you in."

Being tall, blond and blue-eyed, he was obviously an ideal specimen of Hitler's dream-race, the 'Aryan Master Race.' He always remained in the room with me, never saying one word unless it was strictly work-related. Even though he was constantly present, I learned to totally ignore him. I felt, at least during working hours, as though I had the luxury of having my own room within the concentration camp.

The act of guiding my pencil along the drawing board helped me preserve some of my strength. Since this was much less demanding than any other kind of hard physical engagement, I tried to extend my drawing activities for as long as I possibly could. On a few occasions I handed the guard a design that I knew would be rejected when he would show it to his superiors. Naturally, I had to be careful not to overdo this, for fear that my captors might catch onto the game. Eventually, I submitted a layout, knowing that it would be accepted, having now managed to stretch out the precious time that the designing of this piece of furniture afforded me.

Finally I began the actual construction of the desk. Being cautious not to create any suspicion, I was able to maintain a moderate work pace. I soon detected that as long as I was moving my hands, seemingly doing something, the guard would just ignore me. I was not allowed to close the door, however. This bothered me particularly because I could not shut out the constant penetrating drone of the countless machines in the adjoining workshop.

My superman-guard proved to possess some human traits after all! Even he, at least once during the day, had to leave his post to visit the bathroom. Of course, being the dangerous furniture maker that I was, I could not be left unguarded—not even for a minute! To make sure that I remained in my place he would order one of his trusted Polish foremen from the factory to take over his momentarily abandoned position.

This man did not say anything either at first, but the expression on his face was not too unfriendly. Also, he was not wearing a gun as my other 'friend' did. Encouraged by these facts I walked over and closed the door. What a relief! My eardrums had a reprieve! The man would say something in Polish to me and would open the door. I did not understand what he was saying and was certainly not intimidated by him. I went over and closed the door again, only to have him open it once more. His Polish now was mixed with some heavily accented German words. I was still not quite sure what he meant to tell me, but I saw the faint, encouraging smile that played across his face. It almost seemed as though for some reason he was trying to convince me to keep the door open, so I did. I soon had the answer to that puzzle. Suddenly, as one of the Polish women from the factory passed briskly by that open door, a beautiful, shiny red apple rolled along the cement floor towards me. It was extremely risky for her to attempt such a wonderful deed. Yet on a different occasion another apple came rolling through the door. I particularly appreciated this act of sharing because I knew that food rations for the Polish slave-laborers were also extremely restricted under the Nazi occupation of Poland.

My workday lasted for at least ten hours, and afterwards my guard marched me back to the camp. My only regret during this period was that this time I was not able to have my brother join me in the workshop.

In Auschwitz/Golleschau, regardless of what job had been assigned, the meager food rations remained the same for everyone. It was easy to see why we kept on losing weight.

Life within the walls of this small camp was made particularly miserable by two low-life characters. Both were convicted murderers and former inmates of a high-security prison in Germany. These prisoners were among the countless numbers that had been sent to the concentration camps as Hitler emptied the prisons of security guards to free them for military duty.

The SS commander of Golleschau apparently derived demented pleasure from delegating the commanding authority over the entire camp to one of these two despicable characters. He was also provided by the commander with the power to appoint a "right-hand man" to be the Head *Kapo* (a sort of foreman who was usually mean and murderous). What a coincidence! His appointee proved to be his buddy, the other murder convict! The two of them, like a couple of buffoons, wearing their fancy, tailored uniforms, would strut busily about, and also otherwise tried to outperform the murderous SS guards.

We learned quickly that it was a very wise idea to avoid these monsters if at all possible. The slightest incident would send them into uncontrollable rages, turning them into foaming, ferocious animals. Here they were able to practice their deadly, murderous handicraft without having to fear any repercussions.The activity that originally had landed them in prison was here a legalized 'profession.' Fortunately for me, because of my duty in the workshop, I was able to avoid them most of the time.

At the beginning of January, 1945, a fellow prisoner, lowering his voice, muttered, "I've heard that the Soviet troops are beating the Nazi forces in the east and that they are forcing their westward retreat through Poland toward Germany." With controlled excitement, he added, "If this is true, then no doubt their drive will clearly sweep them through these areas! Soon we will be free!" This wonderful news spread like wildfire. So we waited and prayed for the troops to arrive. Our liberation seemed to be imminent!

In anticipation of my liberation I had barely noticed the slightly sore, swollen area that was developing under my left arm. I became somewhat concerned about the state of my health, as the swollen area seemed to be slowly growing. After a few days, I was relieved to see that it began to drain a bit, providing me with some relief and the hope that the apparent infection would now begin to clear up.

During the following week we were able to pick up some far away artillery noises and were hopeful that the Soviet troops had moved closer to the camp. When the order was given to assemble into marching columns and begin the evacuation process of the camp it became clear that our captors had no intention of allowing us to be liberated. Hundreds of non-Jewish prisoners also found themselves part of that huge marching group.

As the time drew nearer for my brother and me to fall into place in one of the marching columns I had the opportunity to speak briefly with another prisoner who was acting as a medic. He thought it would be important for me to keep the draining area under my arm covered, not only while we were marching but also during the time of any expected subsequent transportation. He stuffed a large wad of cotton into my armpit and secured it with a long piece of tape, beginning in the front of my chest, reaching under my arm and ending on the back of my shoulder.

January 18, 1945, was a relentlessly cold winter day. Our long columns of mostly weak and starving prisoners were ordered into motion on the snow-covered ground. Most of us wore only broken shoes or wooden clogs on our freezing, rag-covered feet. With the guards every few yards on our side we were forced to march for nearly three days to the town of Gleiwitz. More than one-half of the prisoners were killed during that horrifying ordeal, which became known as a 'death march.'

Carrying only the one thin blanket that each of us had been issued, we were pushed into open gondola cars, without roofs. In this bitter cold our covers did not even come close to comforting us. During the ride we huddled closely together to seek warmth from each other for our freezing bodies.

The train stopped occasionally, yet we were never allowed to leave that boxcar. At one time we came to a halt right next to a German military train. We stood so close that we could almost touch the train standing on the tracks next to ours. As we looked over the edge of our open gondola, we noticed a German soldier bundled up in heavy winter gear standing on the flatbed railroad car right next to us. From the spigot of a big military kitchen kettle he was filling pitchers with hot, steaming coffee. We watched with longing eyes as he proceeded to fill one container after another. Several containers were now standing right around him, apparently waiting to be picked up. Now it seemed that he was just standing there doing nothing. Hoping to have found a sympathetic soul, we stretched our arms over the rim of our confinement in his direction, our hands holding the empty food bowls that we always carried with us. Looking straight at us with an expressionless face, he simply bent down to open the spigot of the kettle, allowing this precious steaming-hot liquid to run senselessly onto the frozen railroad tracks.

From the direction of the locomotive, a jolting noise started to travel up along our train, reverberating in the stillness of the wintry countryside. When the clanging jolt finally reached our car, we began to roll again. Hours had gone by when, in the darkness of the early morning, I stuck my head carefully over the rim. I recognized with sadness that the train, clattering noisily over the tracks, was slowly passing my old and so familiar home area of Berlin, just four or five blocks away from my old street. After about another two hours we arrived at the concentration camp of Sachsenhausen near Berlin. After two full days of the slow and gruesome ride in the open gondola we were almost relieved to get out of this box. We had the feeling that this would only be a very temporary spot for us.

By now the condition under my arm had become increasingly

uncomfortable. I felt some pain when I held my arm close to the side of my body. I did not dare examine my troublesome spot, for fear that I would have had to remove my bandage and that the tape holding the cotton in place would not stick again. So I left it alone just hoping that it would miraculously heal on its own.We were held there for about five days, after which we were taken to a nearby airplane factory, the Heinckel Werke.

The place we were in now seemed to be a huge, otherwise unoccupied, cold and drafty airplane hangar. We rolled up in our thin blanket and bedded down on the hard cement floor. We had the feeling that this also would only be a temporary stop. Again, I thought it best to wait a little longer before inspecting the ailing spot under my arm.

The elimination of all the concentration camps that were located in the east caused the camps within Germany to become severely overcrowded. The camp commanders did not want to have to feed any more prisoners than they already had. They wanted to get rid of the new arrivals and therefore tried to shove them off on another camp as soon as possible. This is how it happened that once again my brother and I found ourselves in one of the railroad cars on our way to yet another concentration camp.

Here too, the desperation for survival created situations where bullying prisoners stole blankets from each other. Such an extremely violated and endangered prisoner had no choice but to steal one from someone else. The real tragedy here is that the victims of such an act very often were targeted because they were the ones that appeared weak and defenseless. Often they did not have the strength to retaliate. Therefore, their already slim chance for survival was placed in yet greater jeopardy.

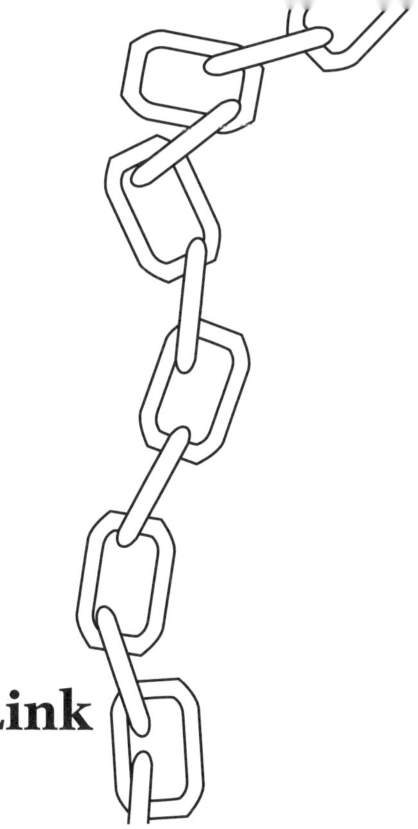

CHAPTER NINE

Eleventh Link

Optimism

During these horrible experiences of camp confinement, we consciously avoided any thoughts or discussions that could lead us to even consider the possibility that survival was impossible. Our nearly unshakeable optimism put all of our trust in our prayers and the absolute confidence that the Allies would be successful in defeating the evil Nazi forces.

We certainly understood why a good number of co-prisoners regarded themselves too realistic to share very much of our optimistic outlook. My brother and I had recognized as an established fact that a defeatist attitude would not be beneficial to our survival. It was of utmost importance to try to dismiss any negative thoughts as soon as they started to form in our minds.

I remember the scene of our arrival at the camp of Theresienstadt. As we took in the foreboding display around us an acquaintance of ours, a man in his middle thirties, put both hands to his face.

With good reason he lamented, "Oh my God, just look at this!

Just look around you! How in the world will we ever make it out of here?"

We saw him every once in a while. It was a sad sight to practically watch this poor man decline before our eyes. He, like many others, apparently had given up all hope.

A prisoner that turned into such a state of deteriorated, blabbering helplessness would be called by the Nazi guards a *Muselmann* (German usage of this word for Muslim. The Nazi application of this word for such a situation clearly reflects their racial and religious disrespect for members of the Muslim faith). They usually would soon be sorted out and taken away to be killed.

For us, the order of the day—everyday—was: "Stay alert, don't enrage any of the guards or the murderous *Kapos*. Wait for the Allied Forces to be victorious."

Twelfth Link

My Profession

I really do not know if it is possible to determine the degree of importance of each of the links individually, for it is obvious that they are clearly intertwined and one would not exist if it were not for the other.

Yet the way I see it, perhaps the most significant of them all was my profession. It had allowed me to exercise my skill in designing and constructing furniture under the most unexpected situations. During inclement weather conditions it provided me with the luxury of being inside, at least during the often required ten to twelve hours of working time. It also gave me the otherwise non-existent opportunity to have a degree of control over my life, providing a degree of freedom in which to determine the pace and intensity of my labor.

Being separated from the groups, sometimes even masses, of co-prisoners created the gratifying feeling of comparatively peaceful privacy. This produced a very welcome sense of relief for me.

At the same time I had to be alert not to awaken any suspicion in the mind of my ever-present guard. Because I could apply my craft in an efficient and directed way I was able to allow my body to burn the sparse caloric content of the meager food rations at a much slower rate. It was also instrumental to my survival that I was spared some of the very long marches to some of the other work locations. The hard labor in stone quarries or on construction sites and the brutal expectations of the guards and *Kapos* were often accompanied by disabling beatings. My professional skills sheltered me for extended times not only during my incarceration in the camp of Theresienstadt, but also during my confinement in Auschwitz/Golleschau.

CHAPTER TEN

Flossenbürg

The concentration camp of Flossenbürg, surrounded by gentle hills of an area known as the 'Oberpfalz,' was located in the northeast of Bavaria, Germany, not far from the Czechoslovakian border. The nearest fair-sized city was Weiden. It had been designed to hold three thousand prisoners when its murderous operation began in May 1938. The camp was created to hold male prisoners only. Its population consisted of a wide variety of people of diverse backgrounds. Among them were non-Jewish political prisoners, homosexuals, Gypsies, prisoners of war of various nationalities, Jehovah's Witnesses and Jews. (It was also the place where the brave Lutheran theologian, Dietrich Bonhoeffer, was executed for his opposition to Hitler.) After withstanding another long and horrifying ride in a frigid boxcar we arrived here on a cold, wintry day, in the beginning of February, 1945.

All along this endless train the heavy sliding doors of the cars screeched as they were pushed open, creating an almost ear-piercing noise, as if they wanted to warn us and discourage our attempt to climb out. Their brief but hideous racket was immediately replaced by the familiar, loud, and just as hideous shouting of the guards and their helpers ordering us to get out. *"Schnell! Schnell!"*

They planted themselves at the door openings. Those not fast enough were unable to escape the accompanying blows of their sticks and gun butts. Herded into the usual marching formation, we were now taken into the camp area. The heavy gates closed behind us.

Again, we had to stand in long lines to have our hair shorn by hand-operated, seemingly toothless, hair-pulling clippers. Following that, hand-pumps blasted us from head to toe with DDT powder, enshrouding us in huge clouds of breath-obstructing dust. This was supposed to kill the ever-present lice and other vermin that were feasting everywhere on our bodies.

The 'check-in' procedures took a long time. It was very late, probably around midnight, when we were divided into a number of groups and finally distributed into the various already heavily occupied barracks. It was pitch-black inside and at first impossible to see anything. As our eyes adjusted a little, we groped our way along the lengthy shelves that were already covered with exhausted, sleeping prisoners. Trying to find an unoccupied spot on which to stretch out proved to be a futile attempt for most of us. There simply was no open space available. We had no choice but to wrap ourselves up in our blankets and stretch out on the hard and ice-cold cement floor.

Because of the abandonment of the concentration camps in the eastern territories, Flossenbürg was hopelessly overcrowded with prisoners that were transferred from those locations. By the time of our arrival the number of inmates here had grown from the original three thousand to well over fifteen thousand.

Very early in the morning we were driven out of the barracks. After long hours of standing in head-count formations it soon became clear to us that there were no work details to be formed. We learned that factories and other labor-requiring facilities outside the camp had been destroyed by Allied bombing attacks.

Our agenda for the day consisted of lining up two or three times for long-lasting head counts or just hanging around in front of our barracks. The gusting, wintry wind made us huddle closely together as in a self-created shelter. For hours we stood with our feet cold and water-drenched on the muddy ground. The soaked sand had frozen during the night, only to return to its previous condition of a melted, mucky mass by early mid-morning.

The soreness under my left arm steadily increased and reminded me that my problem had not disappeared. I now gingerly dared to remove the tape that was holding the wad of cotton in place. I became extremely concerned when I noticed that the opening of the wound was no longer draining and had entirely closed up. This explained to me not only the growing pain, but also the noticeable increase in the size of the swollen area. It began to interfere with my ability to hold my arm close to my body. I now had to extend my elbow slightly away from my body in order to reduce the painful pressure.

This created some additional problems. In the early evenings we were driven back into our barracks. The larger of the two doors usually was kept shut and the narrow opening of the small door would allow only a limited trickle of people to enter. The rest of that large group of prisoners would start to bunch up in front of the door, growing into an increasingly large pack of people.

Those in the rear were subject to merciless beatings by the guards and their helpers, thus driving and pushing everyone forward and toward the entrance. We were driven in like cattle with the usual screaming and cursing. The only way to avoid the battering by the guards was to get to the door as fast as possible. Therefore, the desperate forward pressing motion by the people who tried to dodge the blows in the back was an automatic reaction. When the order had been given to enter the barracks, everyone scrambled to avoid being trapped in that menacing rear position.

Both my brother and I would try to be among the early-entry crowd. Finding myself in the midst of that stampeding mass of pushing and shoving people around me, my arm would be pressed into my side, causing an unbearably excruciating pain. I was forced to make a decision. Based on the choice of the lesser evil, I reasoned that by being in the rear of the pack I would be able to keep my arm away from my body. Yes, I definitely took into consideration the possibility that I might get struck by a blow from our torturers. It was my hope that with a little bit of alertness I would be able to evade the blows here and there. I told Kurt of my decision. He opted to stay with me in the rear. When the stick and gun wielding characters came near us, he would position himself behind me and often catch a blow that was meant for me.

My condition began to deteriorate slowly but steadily. The constant pain and the effects of what seemed to be an obvious infection weakened me noticeably. My brother was always at my side and, as the days wore on and my misery progressed, he often had to assist me in getting around. It was my good fortune, that by this time we no longer were ordered to perform any work details. It would have been impossible for me to survive very long under such conditions. As it was, I tried to draw as little attention to myself as possible.

I had heard that there was a barrack in the camp described as the *Krankenbau* (barrack for the sick.) I understood that it really was available only for 'privileged' prisoners. If one fell into that category, the Block-Elder, who was the SS appointed commander of the barrack, would issue a pink slip as a pass to the *Krankenbau*. Every barrack was under the command of such an assigned 'official.' A brutal co-prisoner, he had placed his bunk comfortably and separately in a den-like corner of the barrack right next to the entrance door. Our Block-Elder was a large man, a Ukrainian political prisoner. Time and time again, he had demonstrated that he was not the greatest friend of Jews, who were by far the greater number of all kinds of prisoners among his 'subjects.'

It was no small wonder that I approached him with the greatest apprehension. Kurt and I had come to the conclusion that my condition was entering a desperate stage. I was in dire need of medical assistance. Perhaps it was possible that I could catch this Block-Elder in a less brutal mood and upon seeing my dilemma, he might hand me that precious pink slip.

As I stood before him, pointing to my arm, without any warning he suddenly slammed his fist into my face. Fortunately, he left me with no more than a sore face and broken glasses. I replaced my glasses from a big bin that was located in a corner and filled to the brim with thousands of eyeglasses. They were part of a collection of eyewear from prisoners that were no longer alive. I went through this mountain of eyewear, trying on dozens of pairs until I finally found some I could get by with. I did not have the nerve to approach this bully again, and for the first time, was at a complete loss as to how I could keep myself alive.

To make things even worse, about three or four days after this incident there was an announcement. We all were to be examined in order to pick out those deemed strong enough to participate in a work detail of one thousand men. Word had it that they would be sent to help with the construction of an airstrip not too far away from this camp.

Kurt, although being very malnourished, was by the guards' standards still in comparatively good shape. We were certain that he would be chosen. We both realized that it would be practically impossible for me to pass by a searching eye without anyone detecting my condition. Yet, it was imperative for me to remain with my brother if I expected to survive. He suggested therefore, that I should attempt to hold my arm as close as possible to my body and try to walk past the inspecting SS doctors holding myself upright and straight.

This day, February 20, 1945, was the worst one in all of my incarceration. My brother was sent one way and I the other. Sadly, I made my way back to the barrack. By evening a good number of the prisoners had been sorted out and sent away. There was now plenty of room in the bunks that night.

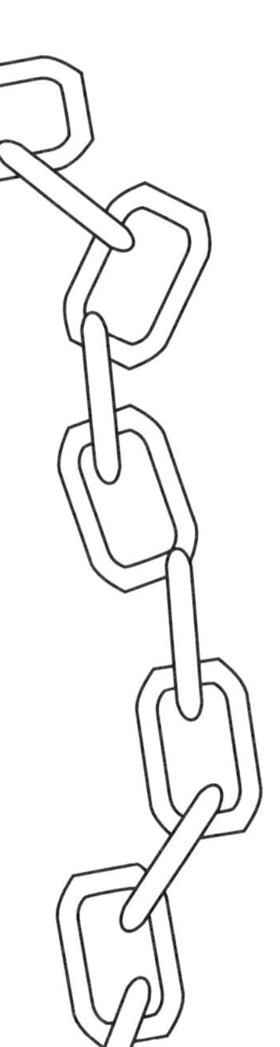

CHAPTER ELEVEN

Thirteenth Link

Brothers Separated

What appeared for us to be one of the most devastating events at that moment became one of the most important links in the chain of my survival. We had been fueled on by a strong need to stay together at all costs. Whenever groups of prisoners were separated from each other we would carefully try to avoid the counting-off procedures that would inevitably result in our being split up. If we had succeeded this time it would never have occurred to me to attempt my next step (link #14) which truly proved to be an act of daring, induced by my sudden utter state of desperation.

I firmly believe that if circumstances had allowed my brother and me to stay together the scenario would have played itself out in an entirely different way. In spite of the sheltering presence and assistance of my brother the infection in my body would have consumed me in a fairly short time. Without any doubt, Kurt's energy would have been drained as he continued to help and support me. Neither one of us would have had enough strength left to overcome the situations that were awaiting us.

A long time after my liberation, I found out that upon our separation my brother was sent to a small satellite camp of Flossenbürg, known as Gannacker, where, out of one thousand prisoners, he was only one of a handful of survivors. A few days before the war had ended, he was part of a remnant group of about fifty prisoners. With his final bit of strength, he was able to escape and for the last few days of the war was sheltered by some wonderful people in a small town of Traunstein in Bavaria.

In retrospect, nothing short of a flash of destiny would have restrained me from joining my brother on his way to Gannacker. Without this link neither one of us would have survived.

There is just no doubt about it!

Fourteenth Link

Desperation

In nearly absolute darkness and without my brother at my side I was stretched out on my bunk. A painful throbbing under my arm kept me from falling asleep, not only depriving me of the blessing of a regenerating rest, but at the same time forcing me to focus on my seemingly hopeless condition.

This sleeplessness, on the other hand, allowed me to analyze my situation. It became quite clear to me that from this point on I was without my brother's help and assistance. With all the other prisoners desperately involved with their own survival, I could not, and did not expect any support from anybody. It did not take too long for me to come to the sobering realization that in my condition the chance to stay alive for any length of time was highly questionable. I had seen too many examples of prisoners in similary hopeless situations.

There was no other possibility! To have any chance at all, I just had to find a way to get to the *Krankenbau* and hope to somehow receive some help there.

But, how in the world would I be able to be accepted there without that necessary pink slip? Approaching that 'block-bully' again would be the equivalent of asking for an execution. A plan slowly started to crystallize in my wakeful mind. I just had to try to sneak out of the barrack in the dark of the early morning, making it necessary to steal past that tormentor who I hoped was asleep in his corner right by the door. I was fully aware of the fact that if I were detected I would be beaten to death.

Surrounded by nearly total darkness, I really had no choice other than to gear myself up and make my move. My bunk was located in the middle of the large barrack. Climbing down from the top shelf with extreme caution I started to make my way toward the big door. As I passed my 'friend' I was relieved to hear snoring sounds coming from the direction of his comfortable single bunk.

The early pre-dawn stillness magnified the sound of the slight creaking caused by the reluctant rusty hinges of the door opening. I was momentarily startled and frozen in my tracks. The snoring had suddenly stopped for what seemed to be an eternally long split-second! When it finally resumed I began to breathe a little easier. I cautiously continued to widen the door's opening just enough to allow me to squeeze through. I was thankful to be on my way without any further encounter.

The barrack that served as a *Krankenbau* in this small camp was easily found. In this case it was marked by a long line of prisoners extending far beyond the barrack, each one holding a pink slip in his hands. I just placed myself at the end of it. I was still waiting in that row as daylight started to take over from the dark. It took hours for the line ahead of me to slowly diminish. The closer I inched my way toward the entrance, the more concerned I became over the lack of that all-important pink slip. I now had become aware of the two men by the door, an SS guard and his helper. Every prisoner, before being permitted to enter, would dutifully hand over his slip to the helper who in turn would pass it on to the guard.

What kind of an excuse could I present for being the only guy in the long line without that piece of paper? I had my serious doubts that I could get by with something like "I must have lost it on the way down here!" What if they ordered me back to my barrack?

How would I manage to get back there without being noticed by the barrack's bully?

I had sneaked out without his permission, and even worse, at a time in the very early morning where nobody was allowed to be outside except with special sanction! Could it be possible that my decision was not only hasty, but also fatal?

While I was pondering this dilemma I had not noticed that I had finally inched my way forward and now had only one person left ahead of me. The helper took the slip out of his hand, gave it to the SS guard next to him and shoved the prisoner through the door.

He started to turn toward me when suddenly another SS guard walked toward the guard and his helper in front of me. They both turned at that moment toward the approaching figure and I made use of that miraculous break to quickly sneak through the entrance. Inside the barrack somebody directed us, according to our impediment to the appropriate treatment area. I now became somewhat less anxious about my situation and was satisfied that at least for the moment I had done all that was possible.

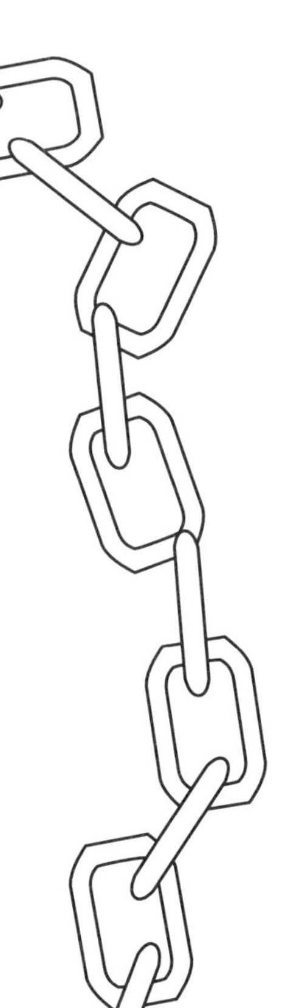

CHAPTER TWELVE

Fifteenth Link

Dr. Schmitz, SS General

I soon found myself in a small room, standing in line behind five or six other weak, sick and emaciated prisoners. Every one of us displayed a very large abscessed swelling that was located on different parts of our bodies. I noticed that one of my co-prisoners had one located on his thigh; another prisoner showed his big lump right on his chest. Two other very gaunt looking people had their lumps situated in the middle of their backs. One person even had his abscess right in the pit of one of his arms, exactly where mine was.

In front of us was a makeshift surgery table, covered with a blue plastic sheet. Next to it stood a very tall Dr. Schmitz, SS General, his uniform covered by a short, white smock. Positioned next to him were two gigantic assistants, chosen obviously from the rank of 'privileged' prisoners.

I had just been pushed into the room when I saw the first sufferer from our line being ordered to place himself in front of the

General. Although it was quite obvious what the problem was, the SS doctor barked at him, asking why he was here.

This wretched, starved-looking man tried to appeal to the doctor's humanity. In a way that reflected his fear and misery, he begged him to help save his life. Cursing at him, this fine representative of the medical profession raised his fist, slammed it into the face of his 'patient' ordering him to "shut up." His two helpers caught the nearly fainting prisoner before he hit the floor, holding him upright between them in a vise-grip position. The doctor took his scalpel, cut and drained the abscess, ignoring the helpless screams from the victim. He wiped the scalpel on what seemed to be a paper towel, covered the wound with a flimsy paper bandage and ordered the next person from our line to come forward. I witnessed this atrocious scene twice, and seriously considered leaving. Sensing the possibility of a likely encounter with the other 'monster' in the barrack, I decided to remain here.

Being last in the line of patients allowed me some time to analyze the situation. I noticed a repetition of the beating scene every time someone would try to make a plea to the humanity of this 'proud member of the master race.' I made up my mind that when it was my turn, to make an attempt to mirror his military demeanor and answer his question in a brusque, military manner, in spite of how miserable and frantically frightened I felt!

I almost regretted that my turn had come. Placing myself between the two big, burly assistants I heard Dr. Schmitz's tersely and arrogantly voiced question, "What is your problem?"

I pointed in the direction of my armpit, and tried to answer in the shortest and snappiest manner that I possibly could muster, "Please, look at this, Herr General." (I played along with his arrogance and over-inflated ego which seemed to make him believe that his SS General status preceded that of an M.D. For that reason I had chosen not to refer to him as "doctor.")

He looked slightly startled, as if he did not expect a prisoner to answer in such a confident manner. He put his hand on my shoulder and said, "Don't worry, my boy, I'll put you to sleep."

I was fully aware of the connotation of this remark. What choice did I have? I had only time to reflect on his comment for a split second. I felt the vise-like grip of his two helpers lifting me like a feather and releasing me rather unceremoniously onto the table. The slight pressure of the ether-cap on my face lessened as the drops of ether did their job to anesthetize me. I woke up feeling the mild slaps on my cheeks that were necessary to bring me out of the anesthetic.

It did not take me long to realize that I now had before me the task of returning to my barrack where I would have to try to melt, unnoticed, into the group of prisoners. At this time of mid-morning everyone was most likely assembled outside.

My mind was starting to contemplate my strategy. Still feeling groggy, I heard Dr. Schmitz instruct his two helpers to find a place for me right in the *Krankenbau*! I was not dreaming!

Dr. Schmitz, SS General, obviously is an important link in the Life-Chain of my survival. His decisions regarding me certainly contributed to my being able to stay alive. To this day and forever, a few unanswered questions regarding this incident remain in my mind: Did he for some reason experience a sudden flash of humanity or charity? Was he just impressed with my ability to control myself? Could it simply have been that he was more willing to be kind at the moment because I was the last person in the line of 'patients' and that he just had a little more time? Was it, perhaps, a combination of all these factors?

I guess I will never know.

CHAPTER THIRTEEN

Sixteenth Link

The Krankenbau (Sick-Barrack)

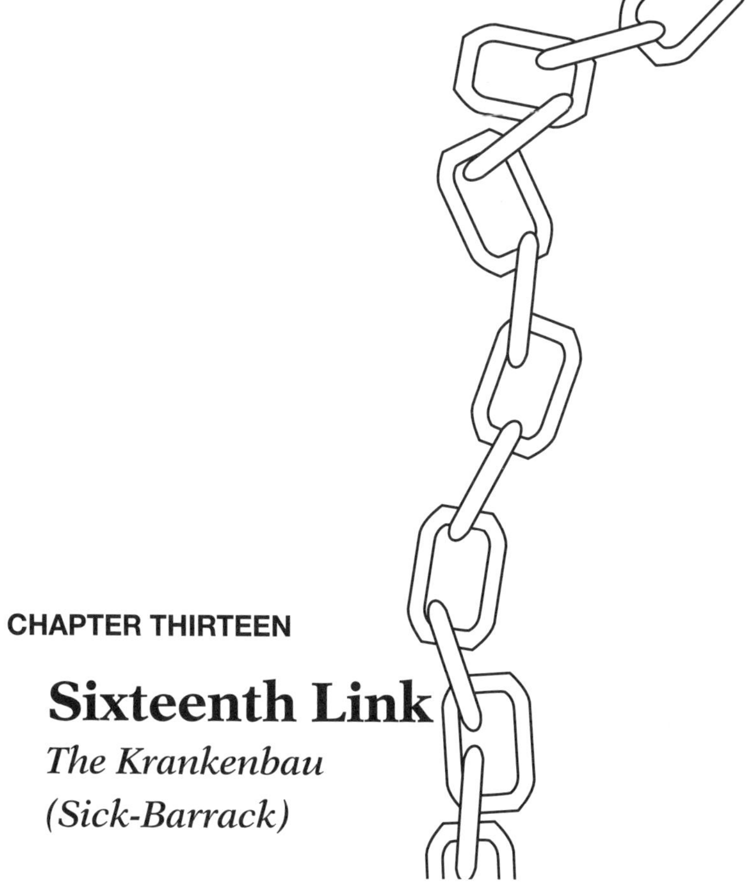

I had to wait quite a while before I was led into a big area, a section of the barrack that was filled with at least twenty individual three-story units of bunk beds. What a relief! I was saved from going back to my original place.

I still felt a little woozy from the after-effects of the surgery and was very much relieved when I was ordered to climb up onto the top of one of the bunks, to at last have the chance to lie down. It was not the easiest task. The numbing effect of the ether had dissipated, and I felt the pain of the freshly cut wound under my left arm. I was not able to see its size because it was covered with a large bandage consisting of nothing but crepe paper. At that time, there was an acute shortage of bandage material. Certainly, it could not be wasted on inmates of the concentration camps. Therefore, rolls of this kind of crepe material were used to cover wounds of such prisoners.

With extreme effort I was finally able to work myself up to the top when I discovered that two other prisoners were already occupying that extremely narrow bunk. One was lying with his feet pointing in one direction and the other in the opposite. I was instructed to place myself in such a way that my immediate neighbor's feet were next to my head. It was very tight but because of our haggard and emaciated conditions it was somewhat manageable. The three of us were covered by one blanket. With disgust, I noticed that it was filthy, and had several dried, hardened spots that were obviously caused by excretions of wounds similar to mine.

Before long, my paper bandage had started to soak through and soon disintegrated. My open wound had not been closed by stitching. The bandage, I presumed, would most likely not be replaced until the next day. That was the moment when I was able to notice that the incision was long enough to reach all the way across my armpit, an incision of four to five inches in length. (The scar under my arm is still easily noticeable.) A medic of some sort did replace my bandage the next morning and I noticed that it lasted a bit longer.

Every mid-morning, Dr. Schmitz, SS General, would make his rounds, strolling regally through the narrow aisles between the bunks of the overcrowded *Krankenbau*, followed by his two obedient subjects. Dressed in his immaculate SS-uniform, he would use the fateful black leather-gloved finger to single out several unfortunate and terribly sick souls. He always passed my bunk seemingly without ever looking at me.

During these selections he announced, "You will be removed from your bunks because you will now be taken to a convalescence facility." The sinister usage of such reference, of course, meant nothing else but the earmarking for immediate extermination.

In spite of the dangerous hygienic circumstances, my wound started to heal without becoming infected. After a few days I could climb out of my bunk and was able to wander around in the barrack where I met all kinds of people. Here, we did not experience the pressures and dangers that were prevalent in the 'regular' barracks. The situation was relaxed.

I even found out that the 'Block-Elder,' overseeing this *Krankenbau*, turned out to be a real human being. My conversation with him revealed that he was a German, non-Jewish, college professor who had opposed the Nazis and was therefore thrown into the concentration camp as a political opponent of the Nazi regime.

One day, after I had regained some of my strength, he approached me and asked if I knew how to cut hair. I suspected right away that if there was a job involved it might qualify me for an extra bowl of soup. After he appointed a few more 'hair-stylists,' he handed each of us a hand-operated hair clipper and sent us on our way to the barracks that prepared new arrivals for the camp. It was the very same situation that we had had to go through when we first arrived.

We placed ourselves in front of the long lines of these hapless newcomers and began wielding our partially toothless clippers. Here too, because of the missing teeth, some of the hair was yanked out, rather than shorn. But, as it was when we arrived, these poor souls felt just as intimidated and frightened as we did at that time. Nobody dared to even whimper. I wished for them as I had wished for myself, that this would be their worst experience in the hellholes that were called "concentration camps." When our work was finished we returned to our places and enjoyed the extra bowl of soup that our 'expertise' had earned us.

Even though my physical condition had improved somewhat, I was certainly fortunate not to have been ordered to return to my original barrack. That I was able to remain in the *Krankenbau* fully deserves the designation of another important link in the chain of my survival.

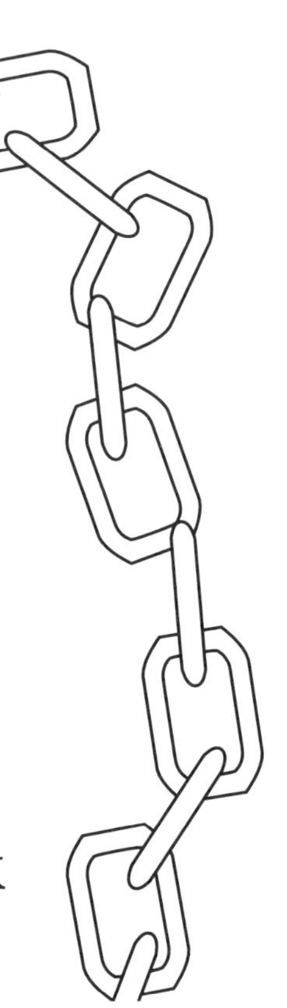

CHAPTER FOURTEEN

Seventeenth Link

Will Kuscheck

During my wanderings through the sick-barrack I became acquainted with Will Kuscheck, a non-Jewish prisoner, who was incarcerated for political reasons. He bunked in a different section of the barrack, a segment that obviously had less confining circumstances that were made available sometimes to "privileged" prisoners. Instead of the usual three-tiered bunk beds, this area was outfitted with only two-tiered ones.

To me it appeared to be utter luxury! And, amazingly, he occupied the upper bunk all by himself. The lower one was usually unoccupied.

I never did ask him to explain to me the reason for his preferential treatment, and he never seemed to be interested in volunteering any such information. Someone told me that he had worked in the camp kitchen until he fractured his leg.

He was a fairly good-sized person. I also noticed that for a camp inmate, he seemed to be in relatively strong physical condition. This could very easily have been due to the extra nourishment surely available to him by working in the kitchen.

The cast on his leg made it more comfortable for him to be stretched out most of the time. He always offered a friendly "hello," as I passed by so that eventually I stopped from time to time to engage him in conversation. His bunk was about chest-high as I stood in front of it when I visited with him. Our exchanges were often interesting and it was gratifying to be able to discuss things not necessarily pertaining exclusively to life in the concentration camps. We talked a lot about our families, our hometowns and our lives before our incarcerations. I was still far away from being very strong but I truly enjoyed those little visits and stopped by as often as I possibly could.

One day we heard something and wondered if our ears were playing tricks on us. Could it be that these occasional, hardly perceptible far away thumps and bangs, by any chance be explosions caused by some kind of artillery? Could the carefully whispered words of the rumor-mill really be true?

Someone, somewhere in the barrack was at times working close enough to the guards. He claimed that he had overheard some concerned remarks about American troops, coming from the west, that were apparently approaching our general area.

These noises, we thought, must be originating from their front lines, from their engagement with the Nazi troops. Somebody yelled, "Shut up for a moment and just listen!" We held our breaths. There was no doubt! Some very distant detonations of bombs were now evident. All of us grew hopefully excited. We expected the American troops to enter our camp at any moment now. This is what we were waiting for during all these miserable years! Our suffering would finally come to an end—we would be free!

Will was finally at the stage where his cast was removed. During one of my visits with him, sometime in the middle of April, 1945, I stood in front of his bunk as we had our usual visit. He was comfortably stretched out when the camp's speaker system suddenly came alive. All Jews were ordered to immediately leave their barracks and assemble outside in marching position.

I said to Will, "I have no idea what this is all about, but I guess I better do as they say. Maybe they want us out of here in order to throw us into different barracks. I am not sure if I will be able to stop by again, so just let us say good bye for now."

Staring at me with a penetrating gaze he firmly said, "Oh no, you are not going to go anywhere! You will stay right here."

I was ready to move and replied, "This is impossible. You know very well that my life would not be worth anything if they found out afterwards that this Jew did not follow their orders."

"Don't you realize that at this point no one can tell one person from another?" Will asked. "Don't you see that most of the prisoners' identification markings have fallen off from their worn, grimy uniforms. Look," he continued, "your own marking, that dirty little yellow triangle (the identification for Jews used in many of the camps) is hanging by its last thread, ready to fall off at any moment."

With that he grabbed it, tore it off, put it in his pocket and remarked, "See, now even I don't know what or whom you are!"

He noticed my indecision. In front of his bunk, right next to where I was standing was an item apparently only available for 'privileged' prisoners, a heavy wooden stool, similar to a tall bar stool.

"You are not going anywhere," he repeated. With one of his vice-like hands he grabbed me tightly by my thin, bony wrist. With his other hand he picked up the wooden stool by the top of one of its legs. He raised and held it well over my shoulder and warned me that it would fall right on my head if I took only the slightest step away from his bunk.

He looked pretty determined and suddenly it all made a lot of sense to me. I stayed with him and observed with sadness the gathering of a huge column of my fellow Jewish prisoners. I was still with him as they were led away out of the camp a short time later.

We had not said a word to each other during all that time. Soon,

Will began to talk. "I can tell you now that I had a very simple reason for trying to force you to stay. I had heard that there were plans to march the Jewish prisoners of this camp from here to the concentration camp Mauthausen." He paused for a brief moment, and then added, "According to my information, they are earmarked to be exterminated."

Records show that the date of the ordered assembly of about 2600 Jews in the concentration camp of Flossenbürg was April 16, 1945. For this unfortunate group it resulted in a combination of death marches and boxcar train rides that lasted nearly a week. Several times the train was attacked by low-flying Allied planes, apparently mistaking it for a military train. Spraying the locomotive and wagons with hails of bullets caused the deaths and wounding of a great number of prisoners.

Will's quick action, keeping me from joining this group, resulted in allowing me to have another four days in which to gather a little more strength. I am convinced that, aside from the risk of being hit by the Allies' bullets, I might not have been able to survive the demands of that lengthy ordeal because of my still weak and emaciated condition.

Therefore, without the restraint forced on me by my assertive friend Will, neither this link nor the next one would exist.

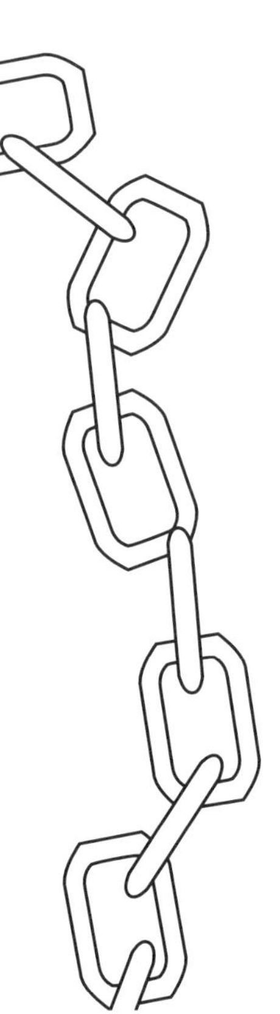

CHAPTER FIFTEEN

Eighteenth Link

General Patton

Another three days had passed. For a day there was a lot of room in the *Krankenbau*, but very quickly it began to fill up again.

It was the early morning of April 19, 1945. For quite a number of days now we knew with certainty that the American troops were nearby. The occasional thundering of exploding bombs and even the burst of machine guns often seemed to be very close. Suddenly, we could hardly trust our eyes as we saw the SS guards rather hurriedly loading their vehicles and rushing out of the camp. We found it hard to believe. Did this mean that we were really free? Nobody dared to leave the camp site for fear of running into any of the guards or German soldiers. Some of the prisoners were dragging out a few white sheets that were left behind in the guards' quarters. They were placing them on top of some of the barracks' roofs after marking them with big letters to indicate to the Allied Air Forces that these were not military barracks.

The firing around us moved closer. We huddled inside, waiting for our liberators to move in. We waited for what seemed to be an eternity. It appeared now as if the sounds of the guns and explosions were subsiding. Were they actually moving away? They were in fact becoming more and more distant. Before we had time to evaluate, the SS guards suddenly reappeared in the camp. Words cannot describe the devastating disappointment that their return represented.

The next morning, April 20, 1945, everyone was ordered out of the barracks to form marching columns of one thousand men each. We were about to set out on what turned out to be for me another 'death march.'

This fiendish system was applied by the Nazis to eliminate as many prisoners as possible, to prevent them from being liberated. For them, the preferential and much simpler solution would have been to kill all the prisoners in the camp sites. But the piles of thousands of dead bodies concentrated in one area would have presented too much evidence to the world.

The great majority of us were by now frail, skeletal creatures. It was a quiet, ghostly-looking procession that had to march at a speed enforced by the guards who were striding along the outside of our columns.

We knew that the American forces were very close and that our liberation could materialize at any moment. Everyone was trying frantically to keep up with the marching pace. Right from the beginning of this ordeal many of the wretched, skin-covered skeletons were far too weak to keep up with the big strides of the Nazi boots. Their debilitated conditions caused them to stumble over the smallest pebble on the road. As they tripped, slumped to the ground or fell too far behind, a shot rang out, often right next to me. Their lifeless bodies were then picked up and thrown onto a truck that steadily followed our pathetic column like a buzzard. The fully loaded vehicle then turned around and drove away to dump the corpses somewhere, while another empty one arrived to take its place.

After nearly three days of marching, the size of our weak, sick and starving marching group had dwindled noticeably. Having received neither food nor water, we were driven back and forth between two flanks of American forces that were in the process of encircling a contingent of German troops. Whenever possible, we tried to pull some dried-up grass from the ground in order to have something for nourishment.

It seemed that I was nearing the end of my strength. I became aware of having difficulty maintaining my balance as flashes of hallucinations appeared before my tired eyes. I had noticed that as a marcher started to hallucinate, he would often lose his balance. This would cause him to weave, which resulted in his fatal stumble to the ground.

I was pulled out of my daze when I heard a voice yelling, "Hey everyone, look over there!" As I turned my head, I noticed the guards fleeing into the nearby woods.

Before me, was the most incredible sight of my life! American armored vehicles were rolling down the hillsides. Through the billowing clouds of dust they kept rumbling forward, passing us as we stopped our labored walking. Out of their turrets, well over our heads, their battle-engaged machine guns kept on hacking away at the German front lines. During all that time the vehicles' hatches were open, from which boxes of military K-rations were flung at us. Everyone scrambled to pick one up. This really was the moment of my liberation!

I finally allowed myself the luxury of lowering my exhausted body to the ground . . . this time, without the fear of being yelled, kicked or shot at! Everyone else was doing the same.

As I rushed to open my box of military K-rations I joyously discovered cans of meat, butter, cheese, crackers and, yes, miracle of miracles, even chocolate! The urge to devour everything at once was simply overwhelming!

Fortunately, my better judgement began to take over, and with some effort I controlled my initial excitement. As my emotions started to simmer down I was able to subdue that nearly uncontrollable desire to wolf down everything in sight. I realized that almost all of this heavenly food was too rich for a starved-out skeleton of skin and bones. I foraged through my wonderful 'horn of plenty' looking for some items that might be a little friendlier to a system that was unaccustomed to nourishing food. I decided to eat a few of the crackers that I found in the box. I just could not resist breaking off a piece of the absolutely delicious-looking chocolate bar!

Regretfully for some, these life-saving boxes that were so well meant were the cause of severe illness and even death. Many of the survivors were unable to muster up enough resistance to fight temptation. Emaciated bodies of sixty-five and seventy pounds were just not able to tolerate most of the rich food these ration boxes contained.

I was still sitting on the ground with my box of treasures on my lap. My eyes were scanning the surroundings. Suddenly, they stopped at a familiar-looking image. There was my buddy, Will, from the *Krankenbau*! We had lost sight of each other when we were ordered out of the barrack. We approached each other happily and sat down together to munch on a few more of our goodies.

The US commander's vehicle appeared and stopped in front of us to give us instructions, announcing his regrets that he had not been able to reach us any sooner. He explained, "Stamsried, the nearby village, is only about a quarter of a mile away. There, the staff of the American Red Cross will be waiting for you. They are prepared to attend to your medical and personal needs."

The liberated men, who were resting all around us applauded, most of them with tears streaming down their sunken cheeks. Some did not even have the strength to raise their frail hands.

The commander added, "Trucks and jeeps will be available for those of you who don't want to walk."

"Oh come on," my mind and body seemed to react, "who would want to walk another step? Who would even be able to do so for that matter? He is just wasting everyone's precious time by making a suggestion like that."

He continued, "Those of you choosing to walk may do so. At any time, you may hop onto any one of our vehicles that are steadily patrolling this short road to Stamsried."

Suddenly, I began to realize that I was now, at last, a free man! The crackers and the piece of chocolate must have started my flow of adrenaline. Does this mean that I can now walk as slowly as I want to? That I can sit down any time and any moment I desire to do so? How about that! Our contemptible guards had finally disappeared.

With this in mind, Will and I realized that for the first time in years we would not have anyone shouting, *"Schnell! Schnell!"* at us. So, with our precious food boxes tucked securely under our arms, we took our first careful steps of freedom in the direction of Stamsried.

Will, who was not quite as emaciated and weak as I was, could have kept on walking this one quarter of a mile without much effort. I however, needed to sit down and take a short rest every few minutes. In spite of it all, I found that I enjoyed each step like a wide-eyed child who has just discovered how to walk.

An American patrolling soldier was steadily driving his jeep up and down that short stretch of the road. He stopped several times trying to coax us onto his vehicle without any success. We were almost sure that he would have already finished his duty for the day if it had not been for us two stragglers. The vast majority of the rescued marchers had chosen to take advantage of the truck transportation.

During our little walk we came by a small pond. What luxury! There was refreshing water with which to wash our hands and faces. A few yards from where I was, close to the shoreline, I noticed a pile of human feces. I took a second look because it appeared as if someone in a fit of sarcastic humor had decided to make use of a 100 mark bill instead of toilet paper. I called Will's attention to this little scene.

We both laughed, and he remarked dryly, "It must be nice to be a millionaire!" It suddenly hit me that now, being a free man, I might be in need of some money. Having been accustomed to dirt and filth, it did not faze me when I gingerly picked that bill off the small pile and began swishing it back and forth in the water to wash it. The sun was shining and I spread it out on the ground to dry while we were taking another little rest. Now I was even in possession of real currency! Life could begin!

We mastered that short distance in nearly four hours. It must have been late in the afternoon when we arrived at the American Red Cross compound. We were approached by a huge African-American soldier wearing the insignias of a medic on his uniform. His face wore a big, friendly and welcoming smile. He said something I could not understand because I did not speak English at that time. I immediately recognized that he did not understand any of my German utterings either. Why in the world was he grabbing at my prized possession, my food box? I was holding tightly onto it with both arms. Nobody was going to take anything away from me now! This man seemed to be quite determined, and he kept smiling. In spite of our linguistic shortcomings I eventually comprehended that for some reason this would be just a temporary measure and that my precious box would be returned to me.

I was shown a bed in what seemed to me to be absolutely luxurious surroundings, a well-equipped field hospital. I had my own bed . . . all for myself!

It was here that my weight was established at eighty-two pounds. After a few days of a very carefully controlled eating program I slowly started to gain some weight. My many painful sore spots began to heal. Little by little I regained some of my strength and soon was able to move about. Almost immediately my huge, smiling medic-friend handed me my ration box.

We received the sad and cold statistical news that during this "death march" of nearly three days, our column of one thousand prisoners had shrunk to less than four hundred survivors. I found out that the statistics pertaining to the other marching columns were pretty near the same.

The date of my liberation was April 23, 1945. What made it so much more meaningful to me was the fact that it happened to be the day of my mother's 52nd birthday. Would I ever see her again? Would I see my brother, his wife, any of my relatives, Rita and any of my many friends ever again?

Because the war was not yet over and war activities were still going on in many surrounding areas, the American Command Post recommended not leaving the area just yet. We certainly would have been allowed to come and go as we pleased, but their suggestion was strictly meant, and taken, as good advice.

The Germans finally surrendered on May 8, 1945. But pockets of sporadic fighting continued. On May 24th our American advisors declared it safe for us to move on.

I now began the slow and difficult journey to reach my hometown of Berlin.

The final connecting link is in place. General Patton's brave and heroic soldiers had done their job well. My liberating troops were the 358th Infantry Regiment of the 90th Infantry Division of General Patton's Third Army.

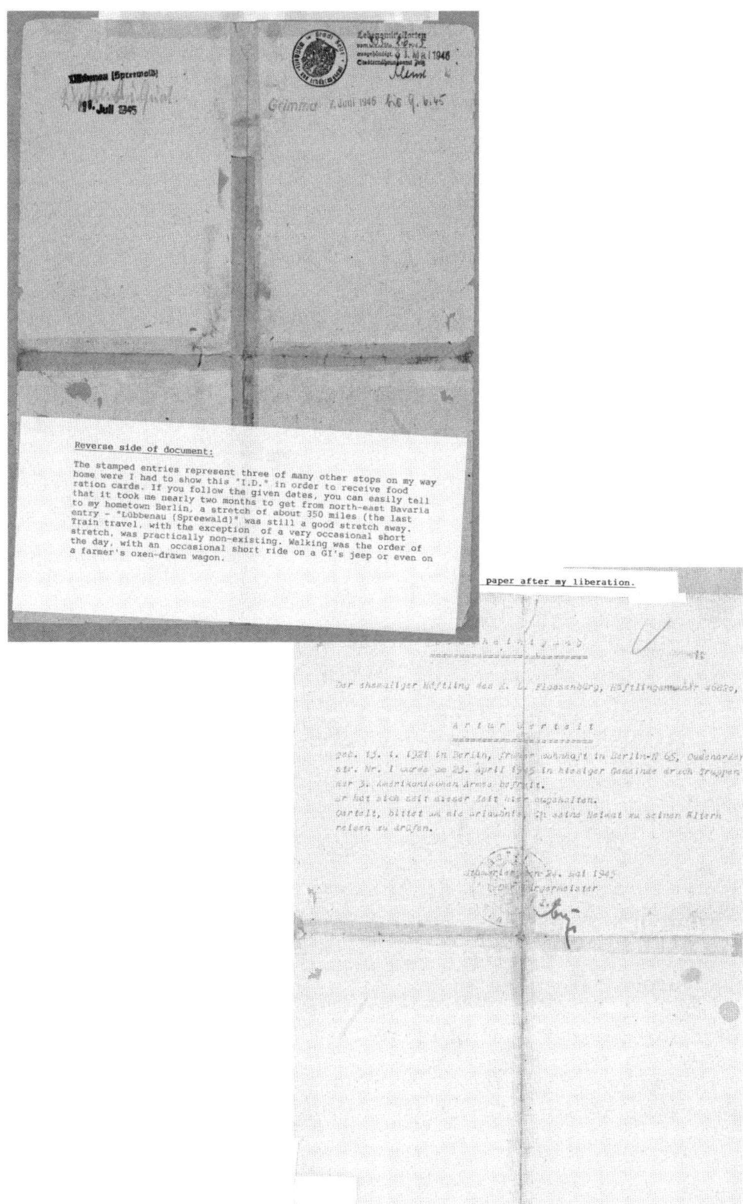

Reverse side of document:

The stamped entries represent three of many other stops on my way home were I had to show this "I.D." in order to receive food ration cards. If you follow the given dates, you can easily tell that it took me nearly two months to get from north-east Bavaria to my hometown Berlin, a stretch of about 350 miles (the last entry - "Lübbenau (Spreewald)" was still a good stretch away. Train travel, with the exception of a very occasional short stretch, was practically non-existing. Walking was the order of the day, with an occasional short ride on a GI's jeep or even on a farmer's oxen-drawn wagon.

paper after my liberation.

Henry's first identification paper after his liberation from the camps (both sides)

Epilogue

Going Home with Will

I found out that getting to Berlin would be a trek of approximately 400 miles northwest of Stamsried. I was anxious to get going. Will told me that his hometown, Forchheim, was located northwest from where we were, only about 65 miles away. He too, was eager to leave our congenial American hosts and we decided to stay together until he had reached his destination. I would then continue on to Berlin.

Long before we left Stamsried, we exchanged our dreadful blue and white striped prisoner rags for civilian clothing. On the morning of Thursday, May 24, 1945, we were issued papers that would identify us as survivors of the concentration camp of Flossenbürg. I was 24 years old at the time. Our instructions were to present this document in order to receive assistance and food items at any official distribution center anywhere on the way to our hometowns. Armed with these papers, we decided to leave right away. Packing a suitcase was not an issue. We had nothing to pack.

The stamped entries on the back represent three of many other stops on my way home where I had to show this I.D. in order to receive food ration cards. The dates shown here identify that it took me nearly two months to get from northeast Bavaria to my hometown Berlin, a stretch of about 400 miles. The last entry – Lübbenau – was still a good distance away.

The war had just ended and all types of transportation had been almost totally destroyed, including the railroad system. We had no choice other than just to keep on walking and walking.

Someone told us that there was a train operating from the nearby town of Schwandorf, for a short stretch of about twenty miles. It traveled northwest to the town of Amberg. No timetable was issued. We just had to wait at the Schwandorf station for many hours until the train was ready to leave. Droves of people had the same idea. By the time we were rolling out of the station, the train was dreadfully overcrowded. Many people were riding on the roofs and others were hanging in clusters on the outside of these old railroad cars. But considering the alternatives, who were we to complain?

The short, slow ride ended much too soon. By now, it was late in the afternoon and we walked, leaving the town behind us to find a farmer's barn where we could spend the night. It was late in May. The weather was mild. We fully enjoyed our freedom to move about as we wished.

It took us another two-and-a-half days to travel the remaining 40 miles to Forchheim. Most of the time we had to walk, but here and there we were able to hitch a short ride on one of the American soldiers' jeeps.

When we finally arrived in Will's hometown, he invited me into his home and asked me to stay with him and his family for a while. Everyone in his family was there. As in most cases regarding non-Jewish political prisoners, the Nazis picked up only the individual 'offender,' unless the other family members were found also to have been involved. Therefore, I witnessed the happy reunion of Will and his family. Could I dare to be slightly optimistic and hope that there would be a similar scene awaiting me upon my return to Berlin?

We had arrived on Saturday morning. The next morning, Sunday, Will was making plans to go to his church. I knew that he was of the Catholic faith. It had been my desire to attend a synagogue to give thanks for my survival, but I was well aware of the fact that all of them had been destroyed during the infamous *Kristallnacht.* I asked Will if he would mind if I joined him in his house of worship. I knew that parts of the service required the congregants to kneel down which my Jewish religion would not permit me to do. I would not want to disturb the worshipers by my non-participation, so I told him that I would respectfully place myself in the last pew of the church. He understood and placed himself right next to me.

Ever since I had seen Will surrounded by his warm family, I had become even more eager to get back to Berlin. Which of my family members would I find had survived? It became increasingly hard to dispel my nagging doubts.

The next day, we parted ways and fondly wished each other farewell. I knew it was time to move on and I felt ready to take my next step toward home.

An Unexpected Encounter

The rhythm of my daily travel routine was generally very similar to the one on the way to Forchheim. One marching day melted into another. There were no trains running anywhere. At times I became so fatigued that I just had to stay in one place for a while to regain my strength.

Many days had gone by and I was finally nearing the eastern part of Germany. The Soviet Union now occupied and controlled this area known as the Soviet Zone of Germany. Berlin was located, like an island, right in the middle of it and had been divided into four parts that were under the jurisdiction of the four Allied powers. Reaching Berlin required me to pass through the Soviet Zone.

Somewhere along the line I had been warned that the Russians would not allow anyone to enter their territory without official transit visas. I was told that in some instances travelers were detained for many days before they received permission to proceed. Some travelers, it was rumored, had even been sent back into the American Zone.

This did not worry me too much because my document stated very clearly that I was a survivor of the concentration camp of Flossenbürg on the way to be reunited with my family in Berlin. I was confident that the number on my arm surely would serve to add some weight to my identification. All of this would make it quite clear that I was not just one of the ordinary Germans or even a former German soldier . . . all of whom they hated so much at that time. This was no small wonder, considering the horrible destruction and mistreatment that the Russians had suffered under the German occupation.

I had now reached the Elster River that currently constituted the border between the American and the Soviet zones of that area. At first, I waited around for a while to study the scene by the river and the actions of the Soviet soldiers on the other side of the bridge. Soon I was joined by a few Germans with the same intentions.

All were a little nervous, and some voiced their concern about possible complications while we hesitantly moved across the bridge toward the Soviet sentries. Each one of us pulled out some kind of paper. One by one, a Soviet officer took the document in his hand and concentrated on it very intensely for what I thought to be a rather long time. He then handed it to one of his comrades. At the same time, he indicated that the paper's owner should move off to the side in order to join the ranks of some of the previous bridge-crossers.

Actually, I was not too concerned because I was confident that the information contained in my document was powerful enough for me to be sent right on my way. I handed my paper to him, but became a little uneasy when he used his index finger to slowly trace the words one by one, line by line, resting the finger on each word for a little while. It suddenly occurred to me that the man just could not read German and therefore certainly was unable to decipher any of our documents. It followed the route of all the other papers and he gave me a little shove toward the small group of assembled people. I did not budge and pointed at the tattooed number on my arm to convey to him that I was a survivor of Auschwitz. It did not seem to register with him at all. He did not give any indication that he understood even a word of my German explanations. A little stronger shove now, accompanied by an unfriendly grunt, suggested to me that this was the end of our conversation.

Forced Labor, Again!

It was now mid-afternoon. Our group of about fifteen people was soon led away in the direction of the cluster of a few barracks ahead of us. This can't be! Am I in a camp again? What is this? One ray of light was that the other Soviet soldiers were somewhat friendlier. They took us around one of the barracks and we now had arrived in front of a huge mountain of potatoes. The soldiers' charades commanded us to each take a seat on one of the simple wooden benches that were circled around that enormous pile. We were each handed a potato peeler. It was our reasonable assumption that this must have been their motive for our internment. Surely, when we have peeled all these potatoes we will be allowed to leave.

"Work fast," we encouraged each other. Even so, a few hours had passed before the huge mountain was eliminated. After we loaded the many big tubs filled with peeled potatoes onto trucks, we were more than ready to bid our unwanted hosts a thankless good-bye.

Instead, we were led into one of the barracks. We received some food and were made to understand that we should each occupy one of the bunk beds. Our protests were ignored, but we were never mistreated.

After three days of performing various chores that always included the potato-peeling job I approached a rather friendly-looking Soviet officer. It appeared that he understood a little German. Again, I tried to communicate my identity to him. He looked at my arm and without saying anything, took me into the office. He handed me my identification paper and said something to the soldier standing nearby who then motioned to me to accompany him. He left me at the gate of the guardhouse. Thankfully marking the end of my potato-peeling career, once again, I was a free man. I am sure that my co-peelers eventually were also released, unless they were under some sort of suspicion.

The Final Stretch to Berlin

Proceeding toward Berlin had not become any easier. Now, being in the Soviet zone, there were no more occasional rides on jeeps. I was thankful that sometimes I could hitch a very bumpy ride on a farmer's oxen-drawn hay wagon. While the speed was not any faster than my walking, it was a relief to be able to rest my feet.

A little more than a month had passed since I left the town of Stamsried. Berlin was finally only about 30 miles away. When I reached the town of Zossen I walked to the demolished train station and saw several cars hitched up to an old, noisy asthmatic steam locomotive. Nobody knew for sure, but rumor had it that its destination would be Berlin.

The railroad system had not yet been reorganized. Tickets were not yet issued. Everybody got on who was able to get on. I had to forcefully squeeze myself into one of the overcrowded compartments. It was a hot day and the compartment reeked of sweat and body odor. We just stood in that position for a long time until the train finally started rolling. It took a few more hours to complete that short stretch to Berlin.

Because of the tremendous, all-encompassing destruction that was caused by the Allied Air Forces, it took me a while to even recognize in which part of Berlin I had arrived. The devastation of the city was bewildering and I was torn apart by two overwhelming emotions, both vengeful satisfaction and painful sadness. On the one hand I felt satisfaction, because the suffering of the city represented to me the logical consequences of a time when people abided by the hateful preachings of that madman, Hitler, and his many followers. There were not nearly enough brave people who dared to oppose him. I only regretted the loss of the many innocent lives. On the other hand I felt painful sadness because I had always loved the city of my birth. There was a tragic time when I began to feel that I was no longer allowed to do so because of the restricting actions of the Nazis.

Our Old Apartment

The four sections of Berlin were known as Soviet, French, English and American Sectors. I proceeded toward the area where we had lived when we were picked up. It was in the part of the city that was now controlled by the French occupation, the "French Sector" of Berlin. We lived on Oudenarder Strasse, a part that was known as Der Wedding, an old labor-oriented area. To my surprise, the sizable, five-story apartment building was still standing. At the time of our coerced departure Berlin was already badly damaged by the Allieds' bombing attacks. The resulting shortage of living quarters for the population was conveniently eased by turning over the Jewish "vacated" premises to "bombed out" Germans. Naturally, first choice was reserved for "well deserving" active members of the Nazi party.

It did not take me long to find out that such a Nazi activist couple had been placed in our fully equipped apartment that we had been forced to abandon. That late afternoon I went to the nearby newly reorganized police precinct's office to dutifully register my return. One of the officers informed me of my right under the new law to demand that my apartment immediately be returned to me.

"Just wait for a moment," he said. "I think I had better escort you over there."

I seemed to detect a trace of gleeful eagerness in his suggestion. A minute later, we were on our way. He mentioned that the people occupying the apartment had been very active members of Hitler's Nazi party. Since he had been involved in a few similar situations, he wanted to warn me not to give in to their possible requests to postpone vacating the premises for a few days.

"Remember how much time they gave you?" I heard him reminding me as we entered the hallway of the building. The policeman's knocking on the second floor apartment door must have been heard all through the building. An elderly couple opened the door. My escort informed them of my legal rights to demand that they immediately vacate the premises. The woman broke out in sobs, heavy tears streaming down her face. She pleaded with me to allow her a few days to have her daughter, who lived out of town, pick them up. She claimed to be all alone with her husband and that they would have no other place to go. My policeman noticed that I was softening a bit. He mumbled something that sounded like, "Henry, don't." By now, it was almost evening and I had made my decision. "Forget about the few days," I warned them as sternly as I could manage. "By tomorrow morning at eight o'clock you had better be out of here!"

My officer shook his head at me, but respectfully enforced my request by remarking that he would return with me. When we arrived the next morning, the door was wide open and the majority of our belongings were gone. The officer looked at me as if to say, "See, didn't I tell you?" Although an attempt was made to track these people down, they had just managed to fade away into the aftermath of the war.

The loss of material items really did not matter much. My thoughts at that moment were much more centered on the concern over the whereabouts of my family. Where were they? Where were my friends?

By now, I should have at least heard about some of them. Since I had my own difficulties returning to Berlin from the camps, I tried to comfort myself with the thought that all I needed to do was wait a bit longer. Most of the other survivors with whom I had spoken were in the same situation. All official buildings had been plastered with various pieces of paper and notes, each asking for information about the whereabouts of someone. It seemed as if the whole world was lost. I added my own notes in various places but to my dismay never received an answer.

July and August passed. I reluctantly arrived at the very mournful and sobering realization that of my whole family I was the lone survivor; not our mother, nor Kurt and Sonja nor her parents seemed to have returned. I had not even heard from my girlfriend Rita or any of her family. None of my many close friends and their families had come back.

It was the middle of September when someone handed me a letter written by Sonja, dated September 10, 1945. Through a mutual acquaintance she had discovered that I was back in Berlin. I was so elated to hear that she had made it. She wrote that she was living in the West German town of Bielefeld and that it would be dangerous at this moment for her to make the over four hundred mile trip to Berlin. It disturbed me greatly when she mentioned in her letter that she desperately hoped that Kurt and our mother had returned to Berlin. Regretfully, I could not provide her with answers regarding them or her parents.

Soon thereafter I received notice that Kurt had fortunately survived and had found out that Sonja was in Bielefeld where he joined her. They notified me that they were going to the city of München (Munich) where they intended to stay for the time being. I was very happy to finally know that at least these two had survived.

Adjusting to New Freedom

It was almost impossible for me to find a job, not even in my trained profession. My faithful friend, Richard, gave me a job in his accounting firm. He did not ask me any questions, but must have soon found out that the adding machine and I were not the best of friends. I am sure that he was not too upset when I found a chance to support myself through my singing ability. An odd combination of various vocal activities enabled me to sustain myself sufficiently until I would be able to emigrate to the USA, which I wanted to do as soon as possible.

I often officiated in services by chanting the cantorial renditions of the liturgy at the newly restored synagogue on the Pestalozzistrasse of Berlin as well as singing in its small choir. I also performed in a quartet of singers who sang at funerals. I did not like this very much, but it paid well and was only meant to be a temporary measure.

A few houses down from where we lived was a butcher shop. Be-

The engagement photo of Henry and his bride, Inge Fromm, taken before their marriage which occurred on September 25,1946.

fore our forced departure we had always gone there, presenting our ration cards, to receive our meager provisions of meat products. (It was soon after the war and all food items were still rationed, except that now our allocation was equal to everyone else's.) The owner, Herr Bohn, never talked much to us. However, once in a while, when no one was watching, he would add a precious extra slice of lunch meat on that otherwise heartless scale of his.

Once again, a few days after my return to Berlin, I went to his shop. As I handed my ration card to him he said, "I know that you once owned a bicycle. I also know that right now, if you wanted to get one, you could not find one anywhere."

I could neither figure out why this conversation started nor where it would lead. He continued, "Did you know that when the Soviets marched into Berlin they grabbed every bike in sight? I was fortunate enough to have had a good hiding place for mine."

He paused, looking at his scale. "It is yours if you do me a favor." He went on to explain, "About 60 kilometers (37 miles) to the east, in the Soviet Zone, live my brother and his family. As you know, at this point one cannot reach anybody. There is still no phone, no mail, and no public transportation available. I am really concerned about their well being. Haven't heard from them for months. If I would bicycle there myself I would hardly be able to get out of Berlin before the Soviets grabbed my bike. But I think with your ID as a Holocaust survivor they wouldn't touch you."

I was in full agreement with his observation and was elated by the thought of coming into possession of a bike again. Besides, to get around in that big city of Berlin was quite cumbersome. Streetcars, buses or the underground took only certain short routes because of the massive destruction of many parts of the city. After 6:00 P.M. all public transportation stopped completely.

He disappeared for a moment and returned with a beautiful, shiny bike. He handed me a piece of paper with the instructions for locating his relatives. "Before you leave, stop here to pick up a little package for them. O.K.?"

The next day I was on my way. It was a nice summer day and I was a happy rider, moving along on a pretty, shady, tree-lined country road. I was by now about 25 miles out of Berlin. In the far distance I began to notice two Soviet soldiers with their guns slung over their shoulders, walking in my direction.

As I came closer I sent a friendly smile and a wave their way. When one of them raised a hand as a signal for me to stop I noticed right away that they were not very congenial. "Of course," I thought again,"with what they experienced from the Germans I cannot blame them too much." I slid off the saddle, standing now on the ground with the bike between my legs. They said something in Russian and I whipped out my tale-telling ID. One of them looked at it with a glazed expression and the other suddenly grabbed the handle bar and gave me a push, obviously trying to get the bike away from me. A little frantic, I pointed to my number on my arm—to no avail. Now both of them started to push me a little harder.

Suddenly, it seemed out of nowhere that a car with a Soviet officer in it appeared. He stopped, and with a commanding voice, said something to the soldiers. Immediately they let go of me. They returned my ID and I tucked it safely back into my pocket. The officer waved me on, and I was on my way.

I arrived without any further incident, encountering a family who was happy with the package I brought and the information about the well-being of their relatives in Berlin. My now slightly shaken self-confidence made me a little concerned about my return trip. It fortunately turned out to be uneventful. I had earned my bike!

On one sunny afternoon I was about to enter a movie theater with a friend of mine, when I recognized two women whose faces looked familiar. One was Frau Erna Fromm who was coming out of the theater with Waldtraut, the younger of her two daughters. I remembered having met them on a few other occasions, particularly at the home of the parents of one of my close friends, Gert Golinsky. This friend and his family had been picked up by the Nazis a long time before we were taken away. Because I was no longer able to visit him, for the last few years I had not seen any of the Fromm family. During our ensuing, brief conversation she invited me to come and visit sometime.

I did not allow too many days to go by. I was eager to hear if she had news about any of our mutual friends. After a bicycle ride of about twenty minutes I entered the building. There was no elevator. Carrying the bike with the bar on my shoulder, I walked up the five stories to the Fromm apartment. I entered and was greeted by a very attractive and familiar-looking young woman. Her name was Inge, the older of the two young and charming sisters. She had certainly changed a lot since I had seen her as a young teenager a few years before at our friend's house. Sheer destiny

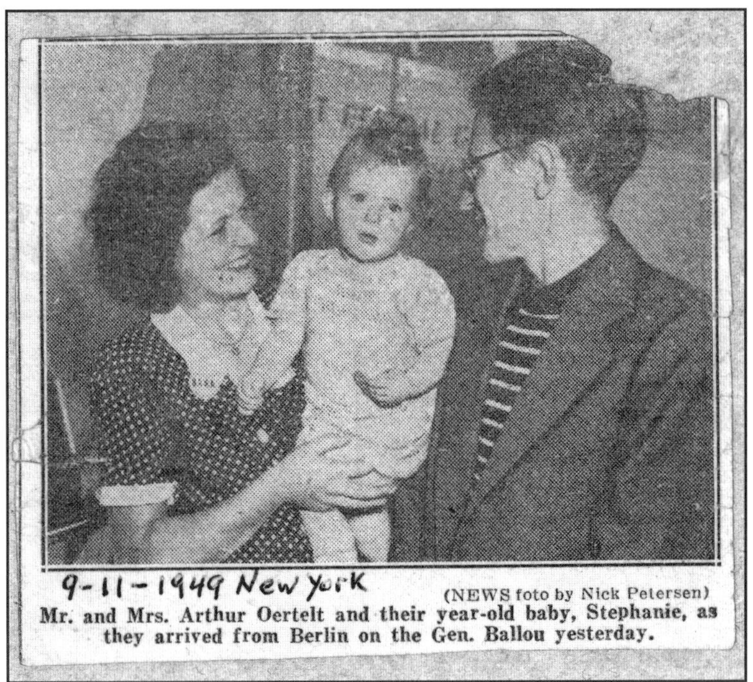

Henry, Inge, and baby Stephanie made the news when they immigrated to America in 1949.

marked this event as the beginning of our 'courting days' leading to our eventual marriage.

Her Jewish mother fortunately had survived her incarceration in Theresienstadt. Because their father was not Jewish, Inge and her sister managed to avoid being sent to the camps. Nonetheless, they overcame many frightening challenges and experienced some incredibly close calls because they were of "mixed" blood (categorized as *"Mischlinge")*.

Regretfully, however, Frau Fromm did not have any information about the fate of any of our friends. Much later I found out that Gert was killed in Buna Werke, a satellite camp of Auschwitz. None of his family members returned from Auschwitz.

Reunited

I wanted to see my brother and Sonja again so I decided to attempt the trip to Munich. This required me to cross the border from the Soviet into the American zone of Germany. I did not get the necessary permission and knew from my previous border crossing that people who were apprehended by the Soviets reported all kinds of incidents of mistreatment. I did not let this worry me too much.

I knew that the winter month of January might not be the most practical time for such an adventure. But since Sonja was now hospitalized in Munich to be treated for tuberculosis, an after-effect of her incarceration in the concentration camps, traveling was impossible for either one of them.

I arrived in the vicinity of the border and had to wait for my contacts to assist me in the actual crossing. My guides never showed up. In the darkness of the very early morning hours, with the help of some local people, I smuggled myself across the border.

A few days later, I arrived in Munich for a joyous reunion with Kurt and Sonja. Our conversations consisted a lot about our horrible past. It felt as if we had just woken up from a frightening nightmare. It was here that Sonja told me what happened in Theresienstadt after Kurt and I were taken away from there. She told me that only about four or five days later there was a big announcement that the wives, mothers and sisters of the deported men could now volunteer to join them. It was suggested that these women would be given the chance to help their men with their work and to care for them. Sonja remembered, "We volunteered in droves, your mother included. Why we believed the story we were told I'll never know—I guess we wanted to believe it." Sonja went on to explain that she was immediately accepted but that our mother was refused because they still needed her in the sewing shop to work on those uniforms.

A few days thereafter all these women with their children were stuffed into terribly overcrowded passenger compartments. They had received small food rations which most of the women wanted to save for their men. When they were ordered out of the train they were forbidden to take anything with them. The meager but precious food items had to be left behind.

When the train finally stopped they had arrived in Auschwitz/Birkenau. On that infamous train ramp women with children were ordered to one side along with the older women. They were told they would be taken care of and did not have to work. As it turned out, their real destination was the gas chambers, followed by incineration in the ovens of the crematoriums.

Sonja, along with the many younger women, was taken into the camp and experienced all the dehumanizing incidents I described earlier. Eventually, she was transported to the concentration camp of Mauthausen, from where she was liberated at war's end.

Through other survivors we found out that our mother had trusted the deceiving promises of the camp authorities. She kept insisting that she wanted to be sent to her sons, and soon succeeded to get herself put onto another transport whose destination turned out to be Auschwitz/Birkenau.

She was suffering from diabetes that needed to be controlled by shots of insulin. This, like any other medication was never available to inmates of the concentration camps. By the time she arrived in Auschwitz her health had very much deteriorated.

We were told that she went with the group of people who were promised medical treatment and temporary work-free conditions. The countless deceptive ploys by the Nazis had worked again. She went the same route other women, children, old and sick people had gone before her, never to return.

The excruciating irony is that in all likelihood she might have survived the remaining six months until the end of the war in Theresienstadt. The work in the sewing shop, it seems, was manageable for her—if for once she only would have recognized the Nazis' fiendish and masterful system of deceit.

We discussed our futures and concluded that we no longer wanted to live in Germany. We hoped to be able to emigrate to the USA. After a few enjoyable weeks in Munich I returned to Berlin.

Longing to Reach the Land of the Free

Inge and I began dating from the moment my eyes met hers. When I went up to their apartment on that visit I had a pair of hard-to-get theater tickets in my pocket, one of which was to be earmarked for another female companion who was just a good friend at that point. I thought it fortunate that I had not yet been able to invite her to accompany me. Hoping that Inge had no other commitments and would be free on Sunday I asked the burning question. With a moment of 'proper' hesitation she agreed.

During the war, the Hebbel Theater in Berlin had lost its roof after being hit by an Allied air attack. It was a cool day in November of 1945. So, outfitted with a blanket, like everybody else, we sat cozily in our seats, listening to and watching the performance of Shakespeare's great creation, *Macbeth.* The walls of the theater surrounded us but we had a beautiful, starry sky above us.

After we were married, it was Inge's and my intention to leave Germany as soon as possible. The French occupational authorities denied permission for anyone to leave their sector for the purpose of immigrating to the USA. The answer to our repeated inquiries as to when their emigration laws would be amended was always "in the near future."

This dragged on for nearly four years. We envied the people who lived in the English or American sectors because we knew that they were able to leave fairly soon after they had submitted their applications.

We decided to move into one of their sectors, only to discover that this would not be permissible unless we found two people from their sector with whom we could trade places. This procedure was called a "head-exchange." There was no one exactly standing in line to take our places in the less desirable French sector and we finally became fed up with the waiting. When we found a man who, for a few dollars, would 'fix' our papers we were able to move to the English sector of Berlin. Right in the middle of all this, July 15, 1948, our daughter Stephanie, our first child, was born.

As survivors of the Nazi persecution we were classified as "Displaced Persons." With this status we became eligible to reach the shores of the USA under a special immigration quota. So soon after the war we had no means to finance such an undertaking. With the wonderful financial assistance of the Jewish Joint Distribution Committee we prepared for our eagerly awaited journey.

This organization reserved the right to distribute their thousands of charges in various areas all over the United States. Given the freedom of choice, most Europeans, including Inge and me, would have chosen the very large cities only, in particular New York City. Of course, at that time we were not aware of their criteria. We were informed that our destination would be St. Paul, Minnesota. Inge and I asked each other, "What and where in the world is St. Paul, Minnesota?!"

In the German harbor of Bremerhaven, on September 1, 1949, Inge, our 14-month-old Stephanie, and I boarded the *General Ballou,* a former troop transport ship. Aboard ship men had to bunk separately from women during the night. Inge and Stephanie shared an unoccupied officer's cabin with another woman and her measles-infected child.

The first three days turned out to be pretty stormy and created a great number of seasick passengers, including myself. I was assigned to a bunk in the forward part of the ship, in the section where its structure slants and narrows to meet at the bow. The heaving walls of the hull quivered with every breaker that slammed noisily into the ship's structure.

I was stretched out on the second-story bunk. I felt so sick that I didn't care if the ship sank or not. I was located close to the open door of a gangway that led to one of the latrines of this troop transport ship. The heavy traffic of loudly moaning and groaning people passing by made it seem as if all the sick people of the entire ship wanted to congregate right in front of my door. The steady and unmistakable sound of vomiting individuals was not particularly helpful for a speedy recovery from seasickness. After three days the sea calmed down a little and I, weakened and hungry, was able to stand on my still wobbly sea legs. Inge was also affected by seasickness, but with little Stephanie next to her, forced herself bravely to attend to the child.

After ten days on the ocean we entered New York Harbor at the beginning of the evening of September 10. The *General Ballou* had now very much slowed down and was almost at a complete standstill when we heard the rumble of the fast-dropping anchor chains that were to secure our ship for the night.

As the dusk of the early evening turned into night, a most spectacular image slowly developed right in front of our eyes! In the midst of bright beams of light, reflected in the gentle waves of the dark waters of the harbor, stood the imposing Great Lady of our dreams, the ultimate symbol of freedom, the Statue of Liberty . . . welcoming us to the shores of the "Land of the Free."

What an imposing greeting it was! What a moving sight for our eyes to behold! Hundreds of awe-struck immigrants streamed onto the deck from their cabins and compartments to show their respect and admiration. People were moving over to the side of the ship in order to get the best view of this amazing spectacle. I was afraid that the ship might capsize because of the nearly one-sided weight distribution. But nobody cared. We stood there with tears in our eyes!

None of us could sleep. The activity on the deck continued throughout the night; the ship remained as busy as an anthill.

Eagerly Embracing the American Lifestyle

The next morning the ship docked and we disembarked. After a two-day stay in New York we headed for St. Paul, Minnesota, by train.

We would have rather remained in New York. For one reason, some close Berlin friends of ours lived there. For another, as large-city people we were not too enthusiastic about living in such a very much smaller city as compared to Berlin. But our authorities instructed us that the organization had set up a budget for our support in case we could not find a job or encountered other problems. They informed us that this budget was not transferable. They would certainly not object to our staying in New York, but we would be totally on our own if we experienced any difficulties. Their very friendly advice was for us to go on to St. Paul for now, and when we were able to take care of ourselves, to move anywhere we wanted. It made a lot of sense. The train brought us to St. Paul. Fifty years later, we are still residing in the St. Paul area and have never regretted it.

We did not know a soul when we arrived in St. Paul. The Jewish Family Service of St. Paul welcomed us warmly and assisted us in getting established in our new environment. One of their representatives, Mr. Lerner, was at the train station at our arrival to pick us up. On the way to our nearby destination his old, and apparently tired car, decided to take a little rest. It was right in the middle of a very busy multi-street intersection, then known as "Seven Corners." While honking cars swerved busily around us, Mr. Lerner's encouraging words in the direction of the engine, accompanied by the grinding sounds of the starter, soon had its hoped-for effect. A few minutes later we were at our destination, which was a room in Mr. and Mrs. Cohen's house on Grand Ave. right next to their tailor shop.

We had hardly put down our suitcases when we had to call a doctor. Our little daughter seemed to have come down with a severe case of measles. She must have contracted it from the child in the cabin on the *General Ballou.*The doctor came (those were the days of doctors making house calls), prescribed some medication, and our little Stephanie started gradually to feel better.

About a week later we transferred to our first apartment. It was all arranged by our welcoming organization, and included used, but nice, furniture. Even a small bouquet of flowers, placed on the dining table greeted us with a colorful smile.

This organization also acquainted us with the "Neighborhood House" on Indiana Ave. at what was then the old "West Side of St. Paul." Its caring director, Constance Currie, made sure that the fairly sizable community of survivor-newcomers had a place to meet. She arranged for programs and a wide variety of all kinds of activities for adults and children. Her many responsibilities also included the administration of the beautiful Red Feather/Community Chest-sponsored summer camp, Camp Owendigo, at Carver's Lake, not far outside of St. Paul. She would make sure that several times during the summer months our group would have the chance to get acquainted with the wonderful phenomena of the American camping and picnicking experience.

I worked at first in my trained profession and Inge took a job working at night. This way, it was possible that our little daughter, Stephanie, would not be attended by strangers. We signed up for classes at the International Institute of St. Paul, becoming familiar with the English language and preparing ourselves for American citizenship.

In our new environment we were fortunate to have met some wonderful people with whom we were able to develop new and close friendships, particularly with the Horts, Mendels, Bliersbachs, Kamps and others. Our similar backgrounds bound us together and our friendships took the place of our missing families. Our Stephanie and Renee (Bliersbach, at that time) grew up like sisters.

At about that time Inge's mother came to the USA, living with us for a few years. She spoke only German, but even the neighborhood children, Stephanie's friends, loved her and they all called her *"Omi"* (Granny).

The next item perhaps belongs to the "It's a Small World" category. Within a few years of our arrival in St. Paul, Inge and I attended a party given by some friends. One of the guests had become somewhat persistent in trying to dig out information about my past. At that time, as was the case with most survivors, I had no desire whatsoever to talk about my history and started to feel rather annoyed by the man's insistent probing.

"You were born in Germany, were you not?" he asked.

"Yes." I answered as shortly as possible, angry that again my accent had obviously advertised my origin.

"Did you serve in the German Army?" he delved in even further.

"No," is all I felt like replying.

As the mostly one-sided conversation continued, he finally extracted the necessary information to find out that I was Jewish and had been incarcerated in several concentration camps.

"I've got to get away from this guy," I said to myself. "Excuse me for a moment. I need something to drink." My faint smile of relief must have faded immediately when I heard him saying, "Great idea, me too."

He followed me to the bar set-up and remained right next to me. I hardly had taken a sip from my drink when he continued his 'interrogation' with another question. "Where were you when you were set free?"

Very reluctantly I found myself replying "I was liberated during a death-march near the camp of Flossenbürg."

Now, with what seemed to be an increasing sense of urgency he asked, "By any chance, did that take place on a road between two small villages called Cham and Stamsried?"

I was stunned! How could he know about these two tiny places in Germany? I had never heard of them before I got there!

Incredibly, this man turned out to be the American officer who had stopped his vehicle in front of our tired marching group of survivors! He was the one that had given us our first directives at the moment of the return of our so long–awaited freedom. He now described the very scene of my liberation to me from his angle. No longer did I feel that he was imposing upon me. His name was Arnold Fink, from St. Paul, Minnesota, an officer in an armored division of General Patton's 3rd Army. We remained good friends until he moved away to another state. I regret that we lost contact many years later.

After five years of residing in Minnesota our dream was finally becoming reality. On Armistice Day (now known as Veteran's Day), November 11, 1954, we were proudly sworn in as new citizens of the United States of America. The year, 1999, was the 50th anniversary of our citizenship. We still celebrate this event every year!

The following year, on October 8, 1955, we delightfully presented Stephanie with David, her brand new baby brother. As it turned out, our dear friends, the Bliersbachs, had the same idea and Renee's baby brother, Chris, was born two years after David's arrival. The boys grew up like brothers.

The good news of our American evolution was about to continue. We were thrilled that one year after our arrival, Kurt, Sonja and their little daughter, Evie, arrived in New York. They soon settled in Portland, Maine, where Kurt accepted a position as cantor. A few years later they also extended their family with the arrival of baby Michael. Our battered and bruised family had started to grow again.

Eventually, Inge was able to quit her night job. I accepted a job as furniture salesman at a fine furniture store, Cardozo's. Six years later I became an insurance agent, a job from which I retired after about thirty years.

Our families have continued to flourish. When the war was over it turned out that Kurt, Sonja and I were the only members of our immediate family to return from the concentration camps. Since our survival, we have always been acutely conscious of the fact that we had been able to thwart Hitler's satanic plans to destroy all the people he hated. This awareness exists for all other survivors as well, Jews and non-Jews alike.

I believe that it was in an act of both resistance and triumph that most of the survivors so eagerly generated new families. Inge and I are fortunate that our two 'kids' married wonderful partners. Stephanie and her husband, Eddie, presented us with two terrific grandchildren, Corey and Paul. David and his wife, Shari, bestowed us with two additional terrific grandchildren, Sarah and Daniel. Paul and Colleen, just recently became the parents of our first great-grandson, Chance.

Kurt and Sonja have also been similarly successful. Their two 'kids' also presented the family with wonderful partners. Evie, who married Duane, gave Kurt and Sonja two terrific grandchildren, Sarah and David. Michael married Lucinda. In August 1998, they presented twin boys, Noah and Issac, to the elated grandparents.

Inge's sister, Waldtraut, who lives in Berlin, married Ernst. Their two 'kids,' Ralf and Susann, have three children between them. They all live in Berlin, but to this day the family has always remained in close contact.

Yes, I was always very busy. This has not changed even in my retirement, but there always was and always will be room in my life for the all-important family. There is even time for traveling, fishing and other joyful activities. Life in America has been very good to us!

It was through my intense involvement with the writing of this book that I became so aware of my past. Until I began to focus on things in a chronological order, I thought that my life, with the exception of my incarceration was almost a normal one. As I kept on recalling and reorganizing everything, I started to regret not having done this sooner.

Retired, my life is almost as hectic as it was during my professional years. I became involved in various organizational activities. One in particular is especially meaningful to me. When Beth Jacob Congregation was founded I was a member of the board of directors. In that capacity I also served on the building committee, assisting in planning for a brand new synagogue.

In Germany I witnessed the horrifying destruction of my and other synagogues. The chance now to actively involve myself, and to watch the step by step creation of a new synagogue meant for me the exciting arrival of a moment in a cycle from destruction to creation! For me, this was gratifying.

My original profession, after having helped me survive the camps, came in handy once more. The sanctuary contains the *ahmud* (podium) that was designed and hand-crafted jointly by two fine craftsmen and me. I personally designed and built the two walnut-wooden holders for the Torah scrolls (the five books of the Hebrew Scriptures).

I am also very busy with lecturing and speaking engagements at universities, high schools and various organizations on the subject of the Holocaust. In the beginning of this book, I mentioned the teacher who had particularly influenced me. She was able to convince me of the importance of informing people, young and old, about the horrible past in order to, hopefully, learn from it. It also is of great significance for me to speak for the voices that no longer can be heard. Furthermore, another of my goals is to show audiences and readers how uninformed the vicious and hateful deniers and critics of the Holocaust are—or choose to be.

It is also very important to recognize that hatred and bigotry destroyed millions of incredibly varied and valuable human lives, representing all races, religions and nationalities. This is true not only in past history, but sadly is still happening in too many places around the world.

It is my greatest hope that through the reporting of the happenings of the Holocaust the world will comprehend that there is an enormous price that we all must pay, with tragic consequences, as a result of standing idly by without providing opposition to hatred and violence of any kind . . . and without lending a helping hand to the persecuted and oppressed. ***"NEVER AGAIN"***

More than 50 years later, the author visited Auschwitz. Most German camps had the sign, "Arbeit Macht Frei" (Work Will Make You Free) at the entrance. It was just another example of typical Nazi sadistic deceitfulness. The trip was sponsored by the Jewish Community Relations Council and the National Broadcasting Corporation.